OpenCV Essentials

Acquire, process, and analyze visual content to build
full-fledged imaging applications using OpenCV

Oscar Deniz Suarez

Mª del Milagro Fernández Carrobles

Noelia Vállez Enano

Gloria Bueno García

Ismael Serrano Gracia

Julio Alberto Patón Incertis

Jesus Salido Tercero

[PACKT] open source ✻

PUBLISHING   community experience distilled

BIRMINGHAM - MUMBAI

OpenCV Essentials

First published: August 2014

Production reference: 1200814

Published by Packt Publishing Ltd.
Livery Place
35 Livery Street
Birmingham B3 2PB, UK.

ISBN 978-1-78398-424-4

www.packtpub.com

Cover image by Arie Leeuwesteijn (aleeuwesteyn@hotmail.com)

Credits

Authors

Oscar Deniz Suarez

Mª del Milagro Fernández Carrobles

Noelia Vállez Enano

Gloria Bueno García

Ismael Serrano Gracia

Julio Alberto Patón Incertis

Jesus Salido Tercero

Reviewers

Nashruddin Amin

Emmanuel d'Angelo

Karan Kedar Balkar

Arturo de la Escalera

Commissioning Editor

Ashwin Nair

Acquisition Editor

Sonali Vernekar

Content Development Editor

Prachi Bisht

Technical Editor

Novina Kewalramani

Project Coordinator

Sageer Parkar

Copy Editors

Roshni Banerjee

Dipti Kapadia

Gladson Monteiro

Aditya Nair

Karuna Narayanan

Adithi Shetty

Stuti Srivastava

Proofreaders

Simran Bhogal

Bridget Braund

Paul Hindle

Bernadette Watkins

Indexer

Hemangini Bari

Mariammal Chettiyar

Tejal Soni

Graphics

Ronak Dhruv

Disha Haria

Abhinash Sahu

Production Coordinator

Kyle Albuquerque

Cover Work

Kyle Albuquerque

About the Authors

Oscar Deniz Suarez is the author of more than 50 refereed papers in journals and conferences. His research interests are mainly focused on computer vision and pattern recognition. He received the runner-up award for the best PhD work on computer vision and pattern recognition by AERFAI and the Image File and Reformatting Software challenge award by InnoCentive Inc. He has been a national finalist at the 2009 Cor Baayen awards. His work is being used by cutting-edge companies such as Existor, GLIIF, TapMedia, E-Twenty, and others and has also been added to OpenCV. Currently, he works as an associate professor at the University of Castilla-La Mancha and contributes to Visilabs. He is a senior member of IEEE and is affiliated with AAAI, SIANI, CEA-IFAC, AEPIA, AERFAI-IAPR, and The Computer Vision Foundation. He serves as an academic editor for the journal PLOS ONE. He has been a visiting researcher at Carnegie Mellon University, Pennsylvania, USA; Imperial College, London, UK; and Leica Biosystems, Ireland. He has co-authored a book on OpenCV programming for mobile devices.

Mª del Milagro Fernández Carrobles received her Bachelor's degree in Computer Science and Master's degree in Physics and Mathematics from the University of Castilla-La Mancha, Spain, in 2010 and 2011, respectively. She is currently a PhD candidate and works at Visilabs. Her research interests include image processing and artificial intelligence, especially in medical imaging.

I would like to thank my parents for their love and support. Without them, I would never have gotten where I am today. I also thank Jorge for his limitless patience.

Noelia Vállez Enano liked computers since childhood, although she didn't have one before her mid-teens. In 2009, she finished her studies in Computer Science through the University of Castilla-La Mancha. She started her work at the Visilabs group through a project about mammography CAD systems and electronic health records. Since then, she has obtained a Master's degree in Physics and Mathematics and has enrolled for a PhD degree. Her work involves using image processing and pattern recognition methods. She also likes to teach and work in other areas of artificial intelligence.

I would like to thank Jose and the rest of my family for all their support throughout these years and specially now that I am writing this book 2200 km away from them.

Gloria Bueno García holds a PhD in Machine Vision from Coventry University, UK. She has experience working as a principal researcher in several research centers, such as UMR 7005 research unit CNRS, Louis Pasteur University, Strasbourg, France; Gilbert Gilkes and Gordon Technology, UK; and CEIT San Sebastian, Spain. She is the author of two patents, one registered software, and more than 100 refereed papers. Her interests are in 2D/3D multimodality image processing and artificial intelligence. She leads the Visilabs research group at the University of Castilla-La Mancha. She has co-authored a book on OpenCV programming for mobile devices.

Ismael Serrano Gracia received his Bachelor's degree in Computer Science in 2012 from the University of Castilla-La Mancha. He scored the highest marks in his final degree project about human detection. This application uses depth cameras with OpenCV libraries. He is currently a PhD candidate at the same university, holding a research grant from the Spanish Ministry for Science and Research. He is also working at the Visilabs group as an assistant researcher and developer on different computer vision topics.

Julio Alberto Patón Incertis graduated from the University of Castilla-La Mancha. He started developing computer vision applications as part of his Master's degree project in Computer Science. He has focused on mobile devices, mainly Android; he has created a mobile application for this platform that is capable of locating, tracking, and recognizing text for blind people. This application was later used as a part of a patent-pending indoor positioning system. OpenCV has been an essential part of all his projects.

Thanks to my parents, as their huge efforts allowed me to obtain a degree at the university. I would also like to thank the Visilabs research group for giving me the opportunity to start developing computer vision applications.

Jesus Salido Tercero gained his Electrical Engineering degree and PhD (1996) at Universidad Politécnica de Madrid, Spain. He then spent 2 years (1997/98) as a visiting scholar at The Robotics Institute (Carnegie Mellon University, Pittsburgh, USA), working on cooperative multirobot systems. Since his return to the Spanish university of Castilla-La Mancha, he divides his work time between teaching courses on robotics and industrial informatics and researching on vision and intelligent systems. For the past 3 years, his efforts have been directed to develop vision applications on mobile devices. He has co-authored a book on OpenCV programming for mobile devices.

To my three precious jewels: Dorita, Juan Pablo, and Jacobo.

About the Reviewers

Nashruddin Amin has been programming with OpenCV since 2008. He enjoys learning Computer Vision topics and writing programs using OpenCV for research purposes. He also maintains a blog (http://opencv-code.com) where he shares his experiences with OpenCV.

Emmanuel d'Angelo is an image-processing enthusiast who has turned his hobby into a job. After working as a technical consultant on various projects ranging from real-time image stabilization to large-scale image database analysis, he is now in charge of developing Digital Signal Processing applications on low-power consumer devices. You can find more insight about his research and image processing related information on his blog at http://www.computersdontsee.net/.

Emmanuel holds a PhD degree from the Swiss Federal Institute of Technology, EPFL, Switzerland, and a Master's degree in Remote Sensing from ISAE, Toulouse, France.

Karan Kedar Balkar has been working as an independent Android application developer for the past 4 years. Born and brought up in Mumbai, he holds a Bachelor's degree in Computer Engineering. He has written over 50 programming tutorials on his personal blog (http://karanbalkar.com) that cover popular technologies and frameworks.

At present, he is working as a software engineer. He has been trained on various technologies including Java, Oracle, and .NET. Apart from being passionate about technology, he loves to write poems and to travel to different places. He likes listening to music and enjoys playing the guitar.

Firstly, I would like to thank my parents for their constant support and encouragement. I would also like to thank my friends, Srivatsan Iyer, Ajit Pillai, and Prasaanth Neelakandan for always inspiring and motivating me.

I would like to express my deepest gratitude to Packt Publishing for giving me a chance to be a part of the reviewing process.

Arturo de la Escalera graduated from the Universidad Politecnica de Madrid, Madrid, Spain, in Automation and Electronics Engineering in 1989, where he also obtained his PhD degree in Robotics in 1995. In 1993, he joined the department of Systems Engineering and Automation of Universidad Carlos III de Madrid, Madrid, Spain, where he is an Associate Professor since 1997.

His current research interests include Advanced Robotics and Intelligent Transportation Systems, with special emphasis on vision sensor systems and image data processing methods for environment perception and real-time pattern recognition. He has co-authored more than 30 articles in journals and more than 70 papers in international congresses.

Since 2005, Arturo de la Escalera has headed the Intelligent Systems Laboratory at UC3M (www.uc3m.es/islab). He is a member of the Editorial Board of the International Journal of Advanced Robotic Systems (topic — Robot Sensors), the International Journal of Information and Communication Technology, The Open Transportation Journal, and The Scientific World Journal (topic — Computer Science).

www.PacktPub.com

Support files, eBooks, discount offers, and more

You might want to visit www.PacktPub.com for support files and downloads related to your book.

Did you know that Packt offers eBook versions of every book published, with PDF and ePub files available? You can upgrade to the eBook version at www.PacktPub.com and as a print book customer, you are entitled to a discount on the eBook copy. Get in touch with us at service@packtpub.com for more details.

At www.PacktPub.com, you can also read a collection of free technical articles, sign up for a range of free newsletters and receive exclusive discounts and offers on Packt books and eBooks.

http://PacktLib.PacktPub.com

Do you need instant solutions to your IT questions? PacktLib is Packt's online digital book library. Here, you can access, read and search across Packt's entire library of books.

Why subscribe?
- Fully searchable across every book published by Packt
- Copy and paste, print and bookmark content
- On demand and accessible via web browser

Free access for Packt account holders

If you have an account with Packt at www.PacktPub.com, you can use this to access PacktLib today and view nine entirely free books. Simply use your login credentials for immediate access.

Table of Contents

Preface

OpenCV, arguably the most widely used computer vision library, includes hundreds of ready-to-use imaging and vision functions and is extensively used in both academia and industry. As cameras get cheaper and imaging features grow in demand, the range of applications taking advantage of OpenCV is increasing significantly, particularly for mobile platforms.

As a computer vision library, OpenCV provides the following two big advantages:

- It is open source and everyone can freely use it, either on an academic level or for real-life projects
- It arguably contains the most extensive and up-to-date collection of computer vision functions

OpenCV is fed with cutting-edge research in Computer Vision, image and video processing, and machine learning.

The first book published on OpenCV provided a mostly theoretical approach, explaining the underlying computer vision techniques. Subsequent books have adopted the contrary approach, filling pages and pages with large examples (almost complete applications) that are difficult to follow. Large examples are difficult to follow and cannot be easily reused in the reader's projects. Examples taking up several pages are simply not appropriate for a book. We believe that examples should be easy to understand and should also be used as building blocks to reduce the time needed to have a working example for the reader's projects. Consequently, in this book, we also adopt a practical approach, although we aim to cover a larger spectrum of functions with shorter, easy-to-follow examples. From our experience with OpenCV, we can affirm that examples are ultimately the most valuable resource.

What this book covers

Chapter 1, Getting Started, deals with the basic installation steps and introduces the essential concepts of the OpenCV API. The first examples to read/write images and video and capture them from a camera are also provided.

Chapter 2, Something We Look At – Graphical User Interfaces, covers user interface capabilities for our OpenCV-based applications.

Chapter 3, First Things First – Image Processing, covers the most useful image processing techniques available in OpenCV.

Chapter 4, What's in the Image? Segmentation, tackles the all-important problem of image segmentation in OpenCV.

Chapter 5, Focusing on the Interesting 2D Features, covers the functions available for extracting keypoints and descriptors from an image.

Chapter 6, Where's Wally? Object Detection, describes that object detection is a central problem in computer vision. This chapter explains the functionality available for object detection.

Chapter 7, What Is He Doing? Motion, considers more than just a single static image. This chapter deals with motion and tracking in OpenCV.

Chapter 8, Advanced Topics, focuses on some advanced topics such as machine learning and GPU-based acceleration.

What you need for this book

The approach followed in this book is particularly suited for readers who are already knowledgeable in computer vision (or can learn the discipline elsewhere) and want to start developing applications rapidly. Each chapter provides several examples of the key available functions for the most important stages in a vision system. The book is, therefore, focused on providing the reader with a working example as soon as possible so that he/she can develop additional features on top of that.

To use this book, only free software is needed. All the examples have been developed and tested with the freely available Qt IDE. The freely available CUDA toolkit is required for the GPU acceleration examples in *Chapter 8, Advanced Topics*.

Who this book is for

This book is neither a C++ tutorial nor a textbook on computer vision. The book is intended for C++ developers who want to learn how to implement the main techniques of OpenCV and get started with it quickly. Previous contact with computer vision/image processing is expected.

Conventions

In this book, you will find a number of styles of text that distinguish between different kinds of information. Here are some examples of these styles, and an explanation of their meaning.

Code words in text, folder names, filenames, file extensions, pathnames, system variables, URLs, and user input are shown as follows: "Each module has an associated header file (for example, core.hpp)."

A block of code is set as follows:

```
#include "opencv2/core/core.hpp"
#include "opencv2/highgui/highgui.hpp"
using namespace std;
using namespace cv;

int main(int argc, char *argv[])
{
    Mat frame; // Container for each frame
```

When we wish to draw your attention to a particular part of a code block, the relevant lines or items are set in bold:

```
#include "opencv2/core/core.hpp"
#include "opencv2/highgui/highgui.hpp"
#include <iostream>

using namespace std;
using namespace cv;

int main(int argc, char *argv[])
{
```

Any command-line input or output is written as follows:

```
C:\opencv-buildQt\install
```

New terms and **important words** are shown in bold. Words that you see on the screen, in menus or dialog boxes for example, appear in the text like this: "Also, the checkboxes labeled as **Grouped** and **Advanced** should be marked in the CMake main window."

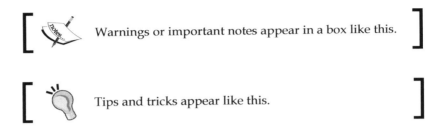

Warnings or important notes appear in a box like this.

Tips and tricks appear like this.

Reader feedback

Feedback from our readers is always welcome. Let us know what you think about this book—what you liked or may have disliked. Reader feedback is important for us to develop titles that you really get the most out of.

To send us general feedback, simply send an e-mail to feedback@packtpub.com, and mention the book title via the subject of your message.

If there is a topic that you have expertise in and you are interested in either writing or contributing to a book, see our author guide on www.packtpub.com/authors.

Customer support

Now that you are the proud owner of a Packt book, we have a number of things to help you to get the most from your purchase.

Downloading the example code

You can download the example code files for all Packt books you have purchased from your account at http://www.packtpub.com. If you purchased this book elsewhere, you can visit http://www.packtpub.com/support and register to have the files e-mailed directly to you.

Downloading the color images of this book

We also provide you a PDF file that has color images of the screenshots/diagrams used in this book. The color images will help you better understand the changes in the output. You can download this file from: `https://www.packtpub.com/sites/default/files/downloads/4244OS_Graphics.pdf`.

Errata

Although we have taken every care to ensure the accuracy of our content, mistakes do happen. If you find a mistake in one of our books—maybe a mistake in the text or the code—we would be grateful if you would report this to us. By doing so, you can save other readers from frustration and help us improve subsequent versions of this book. If you find any errata, please report them by visiting `http://www.packtpub.com/submit-errata`, selecting your book, clicking on the **errata submission form** link, and entering the details of your errata. Once your errata are verified, your submission will be accepted and the errata will be uploaded on our website, or added to any list of existing errata, under the Errata section of that title. Any existing errata can be viewed by selecting your title from `http://www.packtpub.com/support`.

Piracy

Piracy of copyright material on the Internet is an ongoing problem across all media. At Packt, we take the protection of our copyright and licenses very seriously. If you come across any illegal copies of our works, in any form, on the Internet, please provide us with the location address or website name immediately so that we can pursue a remedy.

Please contact us at `copyright@packtpub.com` with a link to the suspected pirated material.

We appreciate your help in protecting our authors, and our ability to bring you valuable content.

Questions

You can contact us at `questions@packtpub.com` if you are having a problem with any aspect of the book, and we will do our best to address it.

1
Getting Started

This chapter deals with the basic installation steps and settings required to develop applications with the OpenCV library. Also, it introduces the essential concepts in order to use the **Application Programming Interface (API)** provided by the library and the basic datatypes supplied. This chapter includes a section with full examples of code that illustrate how to read/write images and video files, and access images from live cameras. These examples also show how to get access to live input from cameras connected to a computer.

Setting up OpenCV

OpenCV can be downloaded from `http://opencv.org/`, and is available for the most popular operating systems, such as Unix (Linux/Mac), Microsoft Windows (Windows), Android, and iOS. In this book, the last stable release (2.4.9) of OpenCV for Windows 7 (SP1) has been used. For Windows, this release comes in the form of a self-extracting archive (`opencv-2.4.9.exe`), which should be extracted to the desired location (for example, `OPENCV_SCR` for `C:\opencv-src`). It should be noted that in Windows it is strongly recommended to allocate the source and binaries at absolute paths without white spaces because errors might appear later.

After extracting the archive, the obtained files are organized in two subdirectories under `OPENCV_SCR`: `build` and `sources`. The first one (`build`) includes precompiled (binaries) versions with Microsoft Visual C++ compilers (MSVC, v. 10, 11, and 12) for 32- and 64-bit architectures (located in the x 86 and x 64 subdirectories respectively). The `sources` subdirectory contains the source code of the OpenCV library. This code might be compiled with other compilers (for example, GNU g++).

Using the precompiled versions of OpenCV is the easiest option and only requires setting the location of OpenCV's dynamic libraries binaries (DLL files) in the **Path** environment variable. For instance, in our setup, this location could be OPENCV_SCR/build/x86/vc12/bin where the binaries compiled with MS VC version 12 for the 32 bit architecture are located. Remember that changing the environment variables in Windows 7 (SP1) can be done on **Advanced System Settings** under **Properties** of **My Computer**. The **Rapid Environment Editor** tool (available at http://www.rapidee.com) provides a convenient way to change **Path** and other environment variables in Windows 7.

This chapter covers a detailed installation process of OpenCV on Windows 7 (SP1). For Linux and other operating systems, you can have a look at the OpenCV online documentation (*OpenCV Tutorials, Introduction to OpenCV* section) available at http://docs.opencv.org/doc/tutorials/tutorials.html.

Compiled versus precompiled library

The OpenCV distribution includes the source code of the library that can be compiled when a different binary version is required. One such situation comes when we need to use the Qt-based user interface functions available in OpenCV (which are not included in the precompiled versions). Besides, the build process (compilation) for the OpenCV library is required if our compiler (for example, GNU g++) doesn't match the precompiled version of the library.

The requirements that have to be met in order to compile OpenCV with Qt are as follows:

- **A compatible C++ compiler**: We use the GNU g++ compiler included with MinGW (Minimal GNU GCC for Windows). This is a standard compiler on Unix and it is appropriate to guarantee code compatibility. Prior to the build process, it is quite convenient to add the location of the compiler binaries (g++ and gmake) to the **Path** environment variable (for example, in our local system, the location is C:\Qt\Qt5.2.1\Tools\mingw48_32\bin).

- **The Qt library**: In particular, the Qt 5.2.1 bundle (available at http://qt-project.org/) is customized for an easy setup because it includes the Qt library and the complete development IDE Qt Creator with MinGW 4.8 and OpenGL. Qt Creator is a full-fledged IDE with free software license that we recommend. The Qt binaries location must also be added to the **Path** environment variable (for example, C:\Qt\Qt5.2.1\5.2.1\mingw48_32\bin).

- **The CMake build system**: This cross-platform build system is available at http://www.cmake.org/. It consists of a set of tools that help the user prepare and generate the suitable configuration files used for building (compiling), testing, and packaging a large code project such as OpenCV.

Configuring OpenCV with CMake

In this section, we illustrate the configuration steps for OpenCV with CMake, with the help of screenshots of the steps involved:

1. The first step involves the selection of directories and compilers. Once CMake is launched, both the source directory (OPENCV_SCR) and the build directory (OPENCV_BUILD) can be set in the proper text fields in the CMake main window. Also, the checkboxes labeled as **Grouped** and **Advanced** should be marked in the CMake main window. We continue clicking on the **Configure** button. At this point, the tool prompts the user to specify the desired compiler and we choose **MinGW Makefiles** using the native compilers. If we choose the **Specify native compilers** option, it is possible to specify a particular location for the compiler and make tools. After clicking on the **Finish** button, the configuration step continues checking the settings of the system. The following screenshot shows the CMake window at the end of this preconfiguration process:

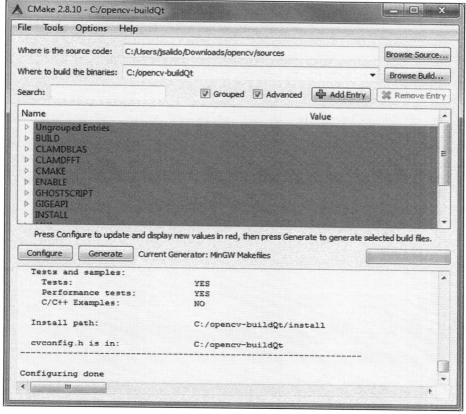

CMake at the end of the preconfiguration step

For the purpose of simplicity, we use in this text OPENCV_BUILD and OPENCV_SCR to denote respectively the target and source directories of the OpenCV local setup. Keep in mind that all directories should match the current local configuration.

2. The next step is the selection of the build options. At the center of the main CMake window, the red entries might be changed if desired. In our setup, we open the entries grouped with the label **WITH** and there we set the **WITH_QT** entry to **ON**, and then we click on **Configure** again to obtain a new set of options.

3. Now, the next stage is to set the Qt directories. In the main CMake window, a few entries are marked in red. These are the required directories to build OpenCV with Qt. The next entries to be set are: Qt5Concurrent_DIR, Qt5Core_DIR, Qt5Gui_DIR, Qt5OpenGL_DIR, Qt5Test_DIR, and Qt5Widgets_DIR (refer to the following figure). In our setup, these directories can be found under C:/Qt/Qt5.2.1/5.2.1/mingw48_32/lib/cmake.

By clicking on the **Configure** button once, we obtain no further red entries and the configuration process is finally done, as shown in the following screenshot:

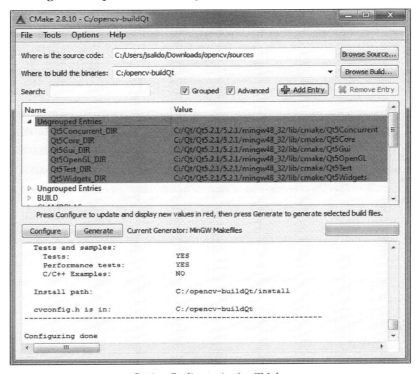

Setting Qt directories for CMake

4. The last step is to generate the project. In this step, we click on the **Generate** button to obtain the suitable project files to build OpenCV in the target platform. Then, the CMake GUI should be closed to continue with the compilation.

In the process just described, it is possible to change the configuration options as many times as desired before the generation step. Some other convenient options to be set are listed as follows:

- **BUILD_EXAMPLES**: This option is used to compile the source code of several examples included in the distribution

- **BUILD_SHARED_LIBS**: Uncheck this option to get a static version of the libraries

- **CMAKE_BUILD_TYPE**: Set this to **Debug** to get a version for debugging purposes and so on

- **WITH_TBB**: Set this option to activate the use of Intel® Threading Building Block that lets you easily write parallel C++ code

- **WITH_CUDA**: Set this option to use processing by GPU through CUDA libraries

Building and installing the library

The compilation should be launched from the console at the target directory (OPENCV_BUILD) set during the configuration with CMake (that is, step 1 from the previous list). The command should be as follows:

```
OPENCV_BUILD>mingw32-make
```

This command launches a build process using the generated files by CMake. Compilation typically takes several minutes. If the compilation ends without errors, the installation continues with the execution of the following command:

```
OPENCV_BUILD>mingw32-make install
```

This command copies the OpenCV binaries to the following directory:

```
C:\opencv-buildQt\install
```

If something goes wrong during the compilation, we should return to CMake to change the options selected in the previous steps. Installation ends by adding the location of the library binaries (DLL files) to the **Path** environment variable. In our setup, this directory is located at OPENCV_BUILD\install\x64\mingw\bin.

To check the success of the installation process, it is possible to run some of the examples compiled along with the library (if the **BUILD_EXAMPLES** option was set with CMake). The code samples can be found at OPENCV_BUILD\install\x64\ mingw\samples\cpp.

Canny edge detection sample

The preceding screenshot shows the output window for the sample cpp-example-edge.exe file, which demonstrates the Canny edge detection on the fruits.jpg input file included with the source OpenCV distribution.

In the next section, we summarize the recipe used to set up OpenCV 2.4.9 in our Windows 7-x32 platform with Qt 5.2.1 (MinGW 4.8).

Quick recipe for setting up OpenCV

The whole process for setting up OpenCV can be done using the following steps:

1. Download and install Qt5 (available at `http://qt-project.org/`).
2. Add the MinGW bin directory (for g++ and gmake) to the **Path** environment variable (for example, `C:\Qt\Qt5.2.1\Tools\mingw48_32\bin\`).
3. Add the Qt bin directory (for DLLs) to the **Path** environment variable (for example, `C:\Qt\Qt5.2.1\5.2.1\mingw48_32\bin\`).
4. Download and install CMake (available at `http://www.cmake.org/`).
5. Download OpenCV archive (available at `http://opencv.org/`).
6. Extract the downloaded archive to an `OPENCV_SRC` directory.
7. Configure the OpenCV build project with CMake using the following steps:
    1. Choose the source (`OPENCV_SCR`) and target (`OPENCV_BUILD`) directories.
    2. Mark the **Grouped** and **Advanced** checkboxes and click on **Configure**.
    3. Choose a compiler.
    4. Set the **BUILD_EXAMPLES** and **WITH_QT** options, and finally click on the **Configure** button.
    5. Set the following Qt directories: `Qt5Concurrent_DIR`, `Qt5Core_DIR`, `Qt5Gui_DIR`, `Qt5OpenGL_DIR`, `Qt5Test_DIR`, `Qt5Widgets_DIR`. Then, click on **Configure** again.
    6. If no errors are reported (marked in red in the CMake window), you can click on the **Generate** button. If some error is reported, the wrong options should be corrected and the **Configure** steps should be repeated. Close CMake after the **Generate** step.
8. Open a console under the `OPENCV_BUILD` directory and run the `mingw32-make` command to start the compilation.
9. If the build process doesn't produce an error, run `mingw32-make install` on the command line.
10. Add the OpenCV bin directory (for DLLs) to the **Path** environment variable (for example, `OPENCV_BUILD\install\x64\mingw\bin\`).

To check the right installation of the OpenCV library, you can run some of the examples included at `OPENCV_BUILD\install\x64\mingw\samples\cpp`.

API concepts and basic datatypes

After installation, preparing a new OpenCV code project is quite a straightforward process that requires including the header files and instructing the compiler to find the files and libraries used in the project.

OpenCV is composed of several modules, grouping related functionalities. Each module has an associated header file (for example, `core.hpp`) located in the directory with the same name as that of the module (that is, `OPENCV_BUILD\install\ include\opencv2\<module>`). The supplied modules with the current version of OpenCV are as follows:

- `core`: This module defines the basic (core) functions used by all the other modules and fundamental data structures, including the dense multidimensional array, `Mat`.

- `highgui`: This module provides simple **user interface** (**UI**) capabilities and an easy interface for video and image capturing. Building the library with the Qt option allows UI compatibility with such frameworks.

- `imgproc`: This module includes image-processing functions that include filtering (linear and nonlinear), geometric transformations, color space conversion, and so on.

- `features2d`: This module includes functions for feature detection (corners and planar objects), feature description, feature matching, and so on.

- `objdetect`: This module includes functions for object detection and instances of the predefined detection classes (for example, face, eyes, smile, people, cars, and so on).

- `video`: This module supplies the functionality of video analysis (motion estimation, background extraction, and object tracking).

- `gpu`: This module provides a collection of GPU-accelerated algorithms for some functions in the other OpenCV modules.

- `ml`: This module includes functions to implement machine-learning tools such as statistical classification, regression, and data clustering.

- Some other less usual miscellaneous modules oriented are camera calibration, clustering, computational photography, images stitching, OpenCL-accelerated CV, super resolution, and others.

All OpenCV classes and functions are in the cv namespace. Consequently, we will have the following two options in our source code:

- Add the using namespace cv declaration after including the header files (this is the option used in all the code samples in this book).

- Append the cv:: specifier as a prefix to all the OpenCV classes, functions, and data structures that we use. This option is recommended if the external names provided by OpenCV conflict with the **standard template library (STL)** or other libraries.

The DataType class defines the primitive datatypes for OpenCV. The primitive datatypes can be bool, unsigned char, signed char, unsigned short, signed short, int, float, double, or a tuple of values of one of these primitive types. Any primitive type can be defined by an identifier in the following form:

```
CV_<bit depth>{U|S|F}C(<number of channels>)
```

In the preceding code, U, S, and F stand for unsigned, signed, and float respectively. For the single channel arrays, the following enumeration is applied describing the datatypes:

```
enum {CV_8U=0, CV_8S=1, CV_16U=2, CV_16S=3, CV_32S=4, CV_32F=5,
    CV_64F=6};
```

The following diagram shows a graphical representation of a single channel (4 x 4) array with 8 bits of unsigned integers (CV_8U). In this case, each element should have a value from zero to 255, which may be represented by a grayscale image.

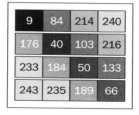

Single channel array of 8 bit unsigned integers for a greyscale image

We can define all of the preceding datatypes for multichannel arrays (up to 512 channels). The following diagram illustrates a graphical representation of three channels 4 x 4 array of 8 bits of unsigned integers (CV_8UC3). In this example, the array consists of tuples of three elements corresponding to an RGB image.

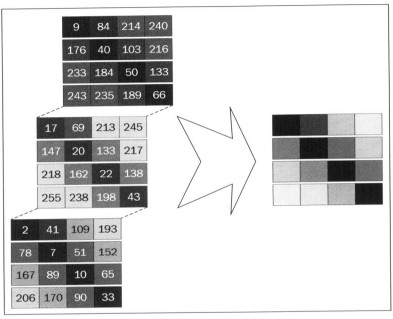

A three-channel array of 8 bit unsigned integers for an RGB image

 Here, it should be noted that the following three declarations are equivalent: CV_8U, CV_8UC1, and CV_8UC(1).

The OpenCV Mat class is used for dense n-dimensional single or multichannel arrays. It can store real or complex-valued vectors and matrices, colored or grayscale images, histograms, point clouds, and so on. There are many different ways to create a Mat object, the most popular being the constructor where the size and type of the array are specified as follows:

```
Mat(nrows, ncols, type[, fillValue])
```

The initial value for the array elements might be set by the `Scalar` class as a typical four-element vector (for the RGB and transparency components of the image stored in the array). Next, we show some usage examples of `Mat` as follows:

```
Mat img_A(640, 480, CV_8U, Scalar(255)); // white image
// 640 x 480 single-channel array with 8 bits of unsigned integers
// (up to 255 values, valid for a grayscale image, for example,
// 255=white)
...
Mat img_B(Size(800, 600), CV_8UC3, Scalar(0,255,0)); // Green
    image
// 800 x 600 three channel array with 8 bits of unsigned integers
// (up to 24 bits color depth, valid for a RGB color image)
```

 Note that OpenCV allocates colored RGB images to a three channel (and a fourth for the transparency, that is, alpha channel) array, following the BGR order with the higher values corresponding to brighter pixels.

The `Mat` class is the main data structure that stores and manipulates images. OpenCV has implemented mechanisms to allocate and release memory automatically for these data structures. However, the programmer should still take special care when data structures share the same buffer memory.

Many functions in OpenCV process dense single or multichannel arrays usually using the `Mat` class. However, in some cases, a different datatype may be convenient, such as `std::vector<>`, `Matx<>`, `Vec<>`, or `Scalar`. For this purpose, OpenCV provides the proxy classes, `InputArray` and `OutputArray`, which allow any of the previous types to be used as parameters for functions.

Our first program – reading and writing images and videos

To prepare the examples for this book, we used the Qt Creator IDE (included in the Qt 5.2 bundle) and OpenCV 2.4.9 compiled with MinGW g++ 4.8 and Qt functionality. Qt Creator is a free multiplatform IDE with very helpful features for C++ programming. However, the user can choose the tool chain to build the executables that best fit its needs.

Our first Qt Creator project with OpenCV will be quite a simple flip-image tool, named `flipImage`. This tool reads a color image file and transforms it into a grayscale image, flipped and saved into an output file.

For this application, we choose to create a new code project by navigating to **File | New File** or **File | Project...**, and then navigate to **Non-Qt Project | Plain C++ Project**. Then, we have to choose a project name and location. The next step is to pick a kit (that is, compiler) for the project (in our case, **Desktop Qt 5.2.1 MinGW 32 bit**) and location for the binaries generated. Usually, two possible build configurations (profiles) are used: debug and release. These profiles set the appropriate flags to build and run the binaries.

When a Qt Creator project is created, two special files (with the .pro and .pro.user extension) are generated to configure the build and run processes. The build process is determined by the kit chosen during the creation of the project. With the **Desktop Qt 5.2.1 MinGW 32 bit** kit, this process relies on the qmake and mingw32-make tools. With the .pro files as input, qmake generates the **makefiles** for Make (that is, mingw32-make) that drive the build process for each profile (that is, release and debug).

The qmake project file

For our flipImage sample project, the flipImage.pro file looks like the following code:

```
TARGET: flipImage
TEMPLATE = app
CONFIG += console
CONFIG -= app_bundle
CONFIG -= qt

SOURCES += \
    flipImage.cpp
INCLUDEPATH += C:\\opencv-buildQt\\install\\include
LIBS += -LC:\\opencv-buildQt\\install\\x64\\mingw\\lib \
    -lopencv_core249.dll \
    -lopencv_highgui249.dll
```

The preceding file illustrates the options that qmake needs to generate the appropriate makefiles to build the binaries for our project. Each line starts with a tag indicating an option (TARGET, CONFIG, SOURCES, INCLUDEPATH, and LIBS) followed with a mark to add (+=) or remove (-=) the value of the option. In this sample project, we deal with the non-Qt console application. The executable file is flipImage.exe (TARGET) and the source file is flipImage.cpp (SOURCES). Since this project is an OpenCV application, the two last tags point out to the location of the header files (INCLUDEPATH) and the OpenCV libraries (LIBS) used by this particular project (for example, core and highgui). Note that a backslash at the end of the line denotes continuation in the next line. In Windows, path backslashes should be duplicated, as shown in the preceding example.

The following code shows the source code for the `flipImage` project:

```
#include "opencv2/core/core.hpp"
#include "opencv2/highgui/highgui.hpp"
#include <iostream>

using namespace std;
using namespace cv;

int main(int argc, char *argv[])
{
    int flip_code=0;
    Mat out_image; // Output image

    if (argc != 4) {//Check args. number
        cout << "Usage: <cmd> <flip_code> <file_in> <file_out>\n";
        return -1;
    }
    Mat in_image = imread(argv[2], CV_LOAD_IMAGE_GRAYSCALE);
    if (in_image.empty()) { // Check if read
        cout << "Error! Input image cannot be read...\n";
        return -1;
    }
    sscanf(argv[1], "%d", &flip_code); // Read flip code
    flip(in_image, out_image, flip_code);
    imwrite(argv[3], out_image); // Write image to file
    namedWindow("Flipped..."); // Creates a window
    imshow(win, out_image); // Shows output image on window
    cout << "Press any key to exit...\n";
    waitKey(); // Wait infinitely for key press
    return 0;
}
```

After building the project, we can run the `flipImage` application from the following command line:

```
CV_SAMPLES/flipImage_build/debug>flipImage.exe -1 lena.jpg lena_f.jpg
```

The following screenshot shows the window with the output image after flipping on both the axes (horizontal and vertical):

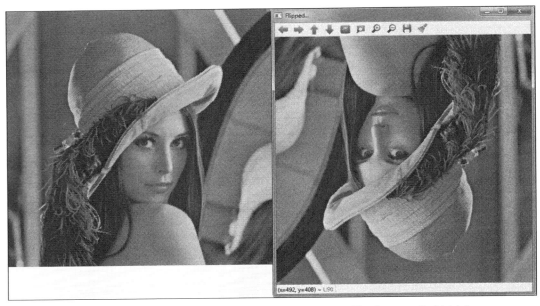

Input image (left) and output image after the flipImage tool has been applied (right)

The source code starts with the inclusion of the header files (core.hpp and highgui. hpp) associated with the modules used by the application. Note that it is also possible to include only the opencv.hpp header since it will in turn include all the header files of OpenCV.

The flipImage example gets the flip code and two file names (for the input and output images) as the command-line arguments. These arguments are obtained from the argv[] variable. The following example illustrates several essential tasks in an OpenCV application:

1. Read an image from the file (imread) to a Mat class and check whether the target variable is not empty (Mat::empty).

2. Call a procedure (for example, flip) with the proxy classes, InputArray (in_image) and OutputArray (out_image).

3. Write an image to a file (imwrite).

4. Create an output window (namedWindow) and show (imshow) an image on it.

5. Wait for a key (waitKey).

The code explanation is given as follows:

- `Mat imread(const string& filename, int flags=1)`: This function loads an image from the specified file and returns it. It also returns an empty matrix if the image cannot be read. It supports the most usual image formats of the files, detected by their content rather than by their extension. The `flags` parameter indicates the color of the image loaded in the memory, which may differ from the original color of the image stored in the file. In the example code, this function is used as follows:

```
Mat in_image = imread(argv[2], CV_LOAD_IMAGE_GRAYSCALE);
```

  Here, the filename is obtained from the command-line arguments (the second argument after the command name). The `CV_LOAD_IMAGE_GRAYSCALE` flag indicates that the image should be loaded in the memory as an 8 bit grayscale image. For a description of the available tags, it is recommended to read the OpenCV online documentation (available at `http://docs.opencv.org/`).

- `bool imwrite(const string& filename, InputArray img, const vector<int>& params=vector<int>())`: This function writes an image to a given file where some optional format parameters are specified after the second argument. The format of the output file is determined by the file extension. In our example code, this function is used without the format parameters as follows:

```
imwrite(argv[3], out_image);
```

- `void namedWindow(const string& winname, int flags=WINDOW_AUTOSIZE)`: This function creates a window without displaying it. The first argument is a string used as a name for the window and its identifier. The second argument is a flag or flag combination, which controls some window properties (for example, enable resize). Next, we show how this function is used in the example using a constant string as a name for the created window, as follows:

```
namedWindow("Flipped ..."); // Creates a window
```

  Compiling OpenCV with Qt adds some new functionality to the `highgui` module (more on that later). Then, the window created with Qt and the `namedWindow` function uses the default flags: `CV_WINDOW_AUTOSIZE`, `CV_WINDOW_KEEPRATIO`, or `CV_GUI_EXPANDED`.

- `void imshow(const string& winname, InputArray mat)`: This function displays an array (image) in a window with the properties set previously with the specified flags when the window was created. In the example, this function is used as follows:

  ```
  imshow(win, out_image); // Shows output image on window
  ```

- `int waitKey(int delay=0)`: This function waits for a key press or the milliseconds specified by `delay` (if `delay` is greater than zero). If `delay` is less than or equal to zero, it waits infinitely. It returns the key code if pressed or `-1` if a key is not pressed after the delay. This function has to be used after creating and activating a window. In the example code, it is used as follows:

  ```
  waitKey(); // Wait infinitely for key press
  ```

Reading and playing a video file

A video deals with moving images rather than still images, that is, display of a frame sequence at a proper rate (**FPS** or **frames per second**). The following `showVideo` example illustrates how to read and play a video file with OpenCV:

```
//... (omitted for simplicity)
int main(int argc, char *argv[])
{
    Mat frame; // Container for each frame

    VideoCapture vid(argv[1]); // Open original video file
    if (!vid.isOpened()) // Check whether the file was opened
        return -1;
    int fps = (int)vid.get(CV_CAP_PROP_FPS);
    namedWindow(argv[1]); // Creates a window
    while (1) {
        if (!vid.read(frame)) // Check end of the video file
            break;
        imshow(argv[1], frame); // Show current frame on window
        if (waitKey(1000/fps) >= 0)
            break;
    }
    return 0;
}
```

The code explanation is given as follows:

- `VideoCapture::VideoCapture(const string& filename)` – This class constructor provides a C++ API to grab a video from the files and cameras. The constructor can have one argument, either a filename or a device index for a camera. In our code example, it is used with a filename obtained from the command-line arguments as follows:

```
VideoCapture vid(argv[1]);
```

- `double VideoCapture::get(int propId)` – This method returns the specified `VideoCapture` property. If a property is not supported by the backend used by the `VideoCapture` class, the value returned is 0. In the following example, this method is used to get the frames per second of the video file:

```
int fps = (int)vid.get(CV_CAP_PROP_FPS);
```

Since the method returns a `double` value, an explicit cast to `int` is done.

- `bool VideoCapture::read(Mat& image)` – This method grabs, decodes, and returns a video frame from the `VideoCapture` object. The frame is stored in a `Mat` variable. If it fails (for example, when the end of the file is reached), it returns `false`. In the code example, this method is used as follows, also checking the end of file condition:

```
if (!vid.read(frame)) // Check end of the video file
    break;
```

In the preceding example, the `waitKey` function is used with a computed number of milliseconds (`1000/fps`) trying to play the video file at the same rate it was originally recorded. Playing a video at a faster/slower rate (more/less fps) than that will produce a faster/slower playback.

Live input from a camera

Usually, the computer vision problems we face are related with processing live video input from one or several cameras. In this section, we will describe the `recLiveVid` example, which grabs a video stream from a webcam (connected to our computer), displays the stream in a window, and records it in a file (`recorded.avi`). By default, in the following example, the video capture is taken from the camera with `cam_id=0`. However, it is possible to handle a second camera (`cam_id=1`) and grab the video from it, setting an argument at the command line:

```
//... (omitted for brevity)
int main(int argc, char *argv[])
```

```
{
    Mat frame;
    const char win_name[]="Live Video...";
    const char file_out[]="recorded.avi";
    int cam_id=0; // Webcam connected to the USB port
    double fps=20;

    if (argc == 2)
        sscanf(argv[1], "%d", &cam_id);

    VideoCapture inVid(cam_id); // Open camera with cam_id
    if (!inVid.isOpened())
        return -1;

    int width = (int)inVid.get(CV_CAP_PROP_FRAME_WIDTH);
    int height = (int)inVid.get(CV_CAP_PROP_FRAME_HEIGHT);
    VideoWriter recVid(file_out, CV_FOURCC('F','F','D','S'), fps,
        Size(width, height));
    if (!recVid.isOpened())
        return -1;

    namedWindow(win_name);
    while (1) {
        inVid >> frame; // Read frame from camera
        recVid << frame; // Write frame to video file
        imshow(win_name, frame); // Show frame
        if (waitKey(1000/fps) >= 0)
            break;
    }
    inVid.release(); // Close camera
    return 0;
}
```

The code explanation is given as follows:

- `VideoCapture::VideoCapture(int device)` – This class constructor initializes a `VideoCapture` object to receive a video from a camera rather than a file. In the following code example, it is used with a camera identifier:

  ```
  VideoCapture inVid(cam_id); // Open camera with cam_id
  ```

- VideoWriter::VideoWriter(const string& filename, int fourcc, double fps, Size frameSize, bool isColor=true) – This class constructor creates an object to write a video stream to a file with the name passed as the first argument. The second argument identifies the video codec with a code of four single characters (for example, in the previous sample code, FFDS stands for ffdshow). Obviously, only codecs actually installed in the local system can be used. The third argument indicates the frames per second of the recording. This property can be obtained from the VideoCapture object with the VideoCapture::get method, although it may return 0 if the property is not supported by the backend. The frameSize argument indicates the total size for each frame of the video that is going to be written. This size should be the same as the input video grabbed. Finally, the last argument allows writing the frame in color (default) or in grayscale. In the example code, the constructor is used with the ffdshow codec and the size of the video capture is as follows:

```
int width = (int)inVid.get(CV_CAP_PROP_FRAME_WIDTH);
int height = (int)inVid.get(CV_CAP_PROP_FRAME_HEIGHT);
VideoWriter recVid(file_out, CV_FOURCC('F','F','D','S'), fps,
    Size(width, height));
```

- void VideoCapture::release() – This method closes the capturing device (webcam) or the video file. This method is always called implicitly at the end of the program. However, in the preceding example, it is called explicitly to avoid wrong termination of the output file (only noticeable when playing the recorded video).

Summary

This chapter started with an explanation of how to build and install the OpenCV library with Qt (using CMake, the GNU g++ compiler, and GNU Make). Then, it is given a quick look to the modules organization of the library with an easy explanation of its basic API concepts. The chapter follows up with a more detailed revision of the fundamental data structures to store arrays and manipulate images. Also, three examples of code, such as flipImage, showVideo, and recLiveVid are explained to illustrate the basic use of the OpenCV library. The next chapter will introduce you to the two mainstream options available to provide graphical user interface capabilities for OpenCV programs.

2
Something We Look At – Graphical User Interfaces

In this chapter, we will cover the main user interface capabilities included with the OpenCV library. We will start with the user interface functions included in the highgui module. Then, we will deal with the insertion of objects (such as text and geometrical shapes) on the displayed windows to point out some specific characteristics on images. Finally, the chapter addresses the new Qt functions included in OpenCV to enrich the user experience.

Using OpenCV's highgui module

The highgui module has been designed to provide an easy way to visualize the results and try the functionality of developed applications with OpenCV. As we saw in the previous chapter, this module supplies functions to perform the following operations:

- Reading images and videos from files and live cameras (imread) through a VideoCapture object.

- Writing images and videos from memory to disk (imwrite) through a VideoWriter object.

- Creating a window that can display images and video frames (namedWindow and imshow).

- Fetching and handling events when a key is pressed (waitKey).

Of course, the module contains more functions to enhance the user interaction with the software applications. Some of them will be explained in this chapter. In the following `tbContrast` code example, we can read an image file and two windows are created: the first one shows the original image and the other is the resulting image after increasing or decreasing the contrast to the original image applying a quite simple scaling operation. The following example shows how to create a trackbar in the window to easily change the contrast factor (scale) in the image. Let's see the code:

```cpp
#include "opencv2/core/core.hpp"
#include "opencv2/highgui/highgui.hpp"
#include <iostream>

using namespace std;
using namespace cv;

int main(int argc, char* argv[]) {
    const char in_win[]="Orig. image";
    const char out_win[]="Image converted...(no saved)";
    int TBvalContrast=50; // Initial value of the TrackBar
    Mat out_img;

    if (argc != 2) {
        cout << "Usage: <cmd><input image_file>" << endl;
        return -1;
    }
    Mat in_img = imread(argv[1]); // Open and read the image
    if (in_img.empty()) {
        cout << "Error!!! Image cannot be loaded..." << endl;
        return -1;
    }
    namedWindow(in_win); // Creates window for orig. image
    moveWindow(in_win, 0, 0); // Move window to pos. (0, 0)
    imshow(in_win, in_img); // Shows original image
    namedWindow(out_win);
    createTrackbar("Contrast", out_win, &TBvalContrast, 100);
    cout << "Press Esc key to exit..." << endl;
    while (true) {
        in_img.convertTo(out_img, -1, TBvalContrast/50.0);
        imshow(out_win, out_img);
        if (waitKey(50) == 27) // If Esc key pressed breaks
            break;
    }
    return 0;
}
```

The following screenshot shows the original image (`fruits.jpg`) and the same image with increased contrast obtained with the `tbContrast` application.

Original image and the image with increased contrast

 To avoid repetition in the examples, only the remarkable new portions of code are explained.

The code explanation is given as follows:

- `void moveWindow(const string& winname, int x, int y)`: This function moves the window to the specified screen (x, y) position being the origin point (0, 0) at the upper-left corner. When a window is created and displayed, its default position is at the center of the screen. That behavior is quite convenient if only one window is displayed. However, if several windows have to be shown, they are overlapped and should be moved in order to see their content. In the example, this function is used as follows:

  ```
  moveWindow(in_win,0,0);
  ```

  Now, the window that shows the original image is moved, after its creation, to the upper-left corner (origin) of the screen while the converted imaged is located at its default position (center of the screen).

- `intcreateTrackbar(const string&trackbarname, const string&winname, int*value, intrange, TrackbarCallbackonChange=0, void*userdata=0)`: This function creates a **trackbar** (a slider) attached to the window with the specified name and range. The position of the slider is synchronized with the `value` variable. Moreover, it is possible to implement a **callback** function for being called after the slider moves. In this call, a pointer to the user data is passed as argument. In our code, this function is used as follows:

```
createTrackbar("Contrast", out_win, &TBvalContrast, 100);
```

A callback is a function passed as an argument to another function. The callback function is passed as a pointer to the code, which is executed when an expected event occurs.

In this code, the trackbar is called `"Contrast"` without a callback function linked to it. Initially, the slider is located at the middle (50) of the full range (100). This range allows a maximum scale factor of 2.0 (100/50).

- `void Mat::convertTo(OutputArray m, int rtype, double alpha=1, double beta=0 ) const`: This function converts an array to another data type with an optional scaling. If `rtype` is negative, the output matrix will have the same type as the input. The applied scaling applied formula is as follows:

```
m(x, y) = alfa(*this)(x, y) + beta,
```

In this code, a final implicit cast (`saturate_cast<>`) is applied to avoid possible overflows. In the `tbContrast` example, this function is used inside an infinite loop:

```
while (true) {
    in_img.convertTo(out_img, -1, TBvalContrast/50.0);
    imshow(out_win, out_img);
    if (waitKey(50) == 27) // If Esc key pressed breaks
        break;
}
```

In the previous chapter, we saw code examples that can create an implicit infinite loop waiting for a pressed key with the function call `waitKey` (without arguments). The events on the application main window (for example, trackbars, mouse, and so on) are caught and handled inside of that loop. On the contrary, in this example, we create an infinite loop with a `while` statement applying the contrast change with the `convertTo` function with a scale factor from `0.0` (slider at `0`) to `2.0` (slider at `100`). The infinite loop breaks when the *Esc* key (ASCII code 27) is pressed. The implemented contrast method is quite simple because the new values for the pixels are calculated by multiplying the original value by a factor greater than `1.0` to increase contrast and a factor smaller than `1.0` to decrease contrast. In this method, when a pixel value exceeds `255` (in any channel), a rounding (saturate cast) has to be done.

In the next chapter, we will explain a more sophisticated algorithm to improve the image contrast using the image histogram equalization.

Then, in the `tbContrastCallB` example, we show the same functionality, but using a `trackbarcallback` function that is called every time the slider is moved. Note that the events are handled when the `waitKey` function is called. The application ends if you press any key. The code is as follows:

```
//... (omitted for brevity)
#define IN_WIN "Orig. image"
#define OUT_WIN "Image converted...(no saved)"
Mat in_img, out_img;

// CallBack function for contrast TrackBar
void updateContrast(int TBvalContrast, void *userData=0) {

    in_img.convertTo(out_img, -1, TBvalContrast/50.0);
    imshow(OUT_WIN, out_img);
    return;
}

int main(int argc, char* argv[]) {

    int TBvalContrast=50; // Value of the TrackBar

    // (omitted for simplicity)
    in_img = imread(argv[1]); // Open and read the image
```

```
                // (omitted for simplicity)
                in_img.copyTo(out_img); // Copy orig. image to final img
                namedWindow(IN_WIN); // Creates window for orig. image
                moveWindow(IN_WIN, 0, 0); // Move window to pos. (0, 0)
                imshow(IN_WIN, in_img); // Shows original image
                namedWindow(OUT_WIN); // Creates window for converted image
                createTrackbar("Contrast", OUT_WIN, &TBvalContrast, 100,
                            updateContrast);
                imshow(OUT_WIN, out_img); // Shows converted image
                cout << "Press any key to exit..." << endl;
                waitKey();
                return 0;
        }
```

In this example, a `void` pointer to the `updatedContrast` function is passed as argument to the `createTrackbar` function:

```
createTrackbar("Contrast", OUT_WIN, &TBvalContrast, 100,
updateContrast);
```

The callback function gets as its first argument the value of the slider in the trackbar and a `void` pointer to other user data. The new pixels values for the image will be calculated in this function.

> In this example (and subsequent ones), some portions of code are not shown for brevity because the omitted code is the same as that in previous examples.

Using a callback function cause a few changes in this new code because the accessible data inside this function has to be defined with global scope. Then, more complexity is avoided on the datatypes passed to the callback function as follows:

- Windows names are defined symbols (for example, `#define IN_WIN`). In the previous example (`tbContrast`), the window names are stored in local variables (strings).

- In this case, the `Mat` variables for the original (`in_img`) and converted (`out_img`) images are declared as global variables.

> Sometimes in this book, the sample code uses global variables for simplicity. Be extremely cautious with global variables since they can be changed anywhere in the code.

The two different implementations shown in the previous example produce the same results. However, it should be noted that after using a callback function, the resulting application (tbContrastCallB) is more efficient because the math operations for the image conversion only take place at the change of the trackbar slide (when the callback is executed). In the first version (tbContrast), the convertTo function is called inside the while loop even if the TBvalContrast variable doesn't change.

Text and drawing

In the previous section, we used a simple user interface to get input values by a trackbar. However, in many applications, the user has to point locations and regions on the image and mark them with text labels. For this purpose, the highgui module provides a set of drawing functions along with mouse event handling.

The drawThings code example shows an easy application to mark positions on an input image. The positions are marked with a red circle and a black text label next to it. The following screenshot displays the window with the input image and the marked positions on it. To mark each position on the image, the user uses has to click the left mouse button over it. In other application, the marked position could be the obtained points or regions from an algorithm applied to the input image.

Next, we show the example code where some pieces of code have been omitted for simplicity, since they are duplicated in other previous examples:

```
    // (omitted for simplicity)
#define IN_WIN "Drawing..."

Mat img;

// CallBack Function for mouse events
void cbMouse(int event, int x, int y, int flags, void* userdata) {

static int imark=0;
    char textm[] = "mark999";

    if (event == EVENT_LBUTTONDOWN) { // Left mouse button pressed
circle(img, Point(x, y), 4, Scalar(0,0,255), 2);
imark++;// Increment the number of marks
sprintf(textm, "mark %d", imark);// Set the mark text
putText(img, textm, Point(x+6, y), FONT_HERSHEY_PLAIN,
                1, Scalar(0,0,0),2);
```

```
imshow(IN_WIN, img); // Show final image
    }
    return;
}

int main(int argc, char* argv[]) {

    // (omitted for brevity)
    img = imread(argv[1]); //open and read the image
    // (omitted for brevity)
    namedWindow(IN_WIN);
    setMouseCallback(IN_WIN, cbMouse, NULL);
    imshow(IN_WIN, img);
    cout << "Pres any key to exit..." << endl;
    waitKey();
    return 0;
}
```

The code explanation is given as follows:

- void setMouseCallback(const string& winname, MouseCallback onMouse, void* userdata=0): This function sets an event mouse handler for the specified window. In this function, the second argument is the callback function executed whenever a mouse event occurs. The final argument is a void pointer to the data passed as argument to that function. In our code, this function is used as follows:

  ```
  setMouseCallback(IN_WIN, cbMouse, NULL);
  ```

  In this case, rather than use a global variable for the name of the window, a defined symbol with global scope has been preferred (IN_WIN).

Image with circles and text on it

The mouse handler itself is declared as follows:

```
void cbMouse(int event, int x, int y, int flags, void*
  userdata)
```

Here, event indicates the mouse event type, x and y are the coordinates for the location of the event at the window, and flags is the specific condition whenever an event occurs. In this example, the unique captured mouse event is the left mouse click (EVENT_LBUTTONDOWN).

The following enumerations define the events and flags handled in the mouse callback functions:

```
enum{
    EVENT_MOUSEMOVE          =0,
        EVENT_LBUTTONDOWN        =1,
        EVENT_RBUTTONDOWN        =2,
        EVENT_MBUTTONDOWN        =3,
        EVENT_LBUTTONUP          =4,
        EVENT_RBUTTONUP          =5,
        EVENT_MBUTTONUP          =6,
        EVENT_LBUTTONDBLCLK      =7,
        EVENT_RBUTTONDBLCLK      =8,
        EVENT_MBUTTONDBLCLK      =9};

enum {
        EVENT_FLAG_LBUTTON       =1,
        EVENT_FLAG_RBUTTON       =2,
        EVENT_FLAG_MBUTTON       =4,
        EVENT_FLAG_CTRLKEY       =8,
        EVENT_FLAG_SHIFTKEY      =16,
        EVENT_FLAG_ALTKEY        =32};
```

- `void circle(Mat& img, Point center, int radius, const Scalar& color, int thickness=1, int lineType=8, int shift=0)`: This function draws a circle over the image with the specified `radius` (in pixels) and `color` at the position marked by its `center`. Moreover, a `thickness` value for the line and other additional parameters can be set. The usage of this function in the example is as follows:

```
circle(img, Point(x, y), 4, Scalar(0,0,255), 2);
```

The center of the circle is the point where the mouse is clicked. The radius has 4 pixels and the color is pure red (`Scalar(0, 0, 255)`) with a line thickness of 2 pixels.

Remember that OpenCV uses a BGR color scheme and the `Scalar` class is used to represent the three (or four if opacity channel is considered) channels of each pixel with greater values for a brighter one (or more opaque).

Other drawing functions included in the `highgui` module allow us to draw ellipses, lines, rectangles, and polygons.

- `void putText(Mat& image, const string& text, Point org, int fontFace, double fontScale, Scalar color, int thickness=1, int lineType=8, bool bottomLeftOrigin=false)`: This function draws a `text` string in the `image` at the specified position (`org`) with the properties set by the arguments `fontFace`, `fontScale`, `color`, `thickness`, and `lineType`. It is possible to set the coordinates origin at the bottom-left corner with the last argument (`bottomLeftOrigin`). In the example, this function is used as follows:

```
imark++; // Increment the number of marks
sprintf(textm, "mark %d", imark); // Set the mark text
putText(img, textm, Point(x+6, y), FONT_HERSHEY_PLAIN,
1.0, Scalar(0,0,0),2);
```

In the `drawThings` example, we draw a text "mark" followed by an increasing number that points out the mark order. To store the mark order, we used a `static` variable (`imark`) that maintains its value between the calls. The `putText` function draws the text at the location where the mouse click occurs with a 6-pixels shift on x axis. The font face is specified by the flag `FONT_HERSHEY_PLAIN` and is drawn without scale (`1.0`), black color (`Scalar(0, 0, 0)`), and 2 pixels thickness.

The available flags for the font face are defined by the enumeration:

```
enum{
    FONT_HERSHEY_SIMPLEX = 0,
    FONT_HERSHEY_PLAIN = 1,
    FONT_HERSHEY_DUPLEX = 2,
    FONT_HERSHEY_COMPLEX = 3,
    FONT_HERSHEY_TRIPLEX = 4,
    FONT_HERSHEY_COMPLEX_SMALL = 5,
    FONT_HERSHEY_SCRIPT_SIMPLEX = 6,
    FONT_HERSHEY_SCRIPT_COMPLEX = 7,
    FONT_ITALIC = 16};
```

Selecting regions

Many computer vision applications require to focus interest inside local regions of the images. In that case, it is a very useful user tool to select the desired **regions of interest (ROI)**. In the `drawRs` example, we show how to select, with the mouse, rectangular regions in the image to locally increase the contrast inside these regions (as shown in the following screenshot). For better control over region selection, we implement a click-and-drag behavior to reshape the rectangular boundary of each region.

Output image with increased contrast in some rectangular regions

For the sake of simplicity, only the code corresponding to the function callback for mouse events is shown, since the rest is quite similar in the previous examples. The code is as follows:

```
void cbMouse(int event, int x, int y, int flags, void* userdata) {

    static Point p1, p2; // Static vars hold values between calls
    static bool p2set = false;

    if (event == EVENT_LBUTTONDOWN) { // Left mouse button pressed
```

```
        p1 = Point(x, y); // Set orig. point
        p2set = false;
    } else if (event == EVENT_MOUSEMOVE &&
  flags == EVENT_FLAG_LBUTTON) {
        if (x >orig_img.size().width) // Check out of bounds
            x = orig_img.size().width;
        else if (x < 0)
            x = 0;
        if (y >orig_img.size().height) // Check out of bounds
            y = orig_img.size().height;
        else if (y < 0)
            y = 0;
        p2 = Point(x, y); // Set final point
        p2set = true;
    orig_img.copyTo(tmp_img); // Copy orig. to temp. image
    rectangle(tmp_img, p1, p2, Scalar(0, 0, 255));
        imshow(IN_WIN, tmp_img); // Draw temporal image with rect.
    } else if (event == EVENT_LBUTTONUP && p2set) {
    Mat submat = orig_img(Rect(p1, p2)); // Set region
        submat.convertTo(submat, -1, 2.0); // Compute contrast
      rectangle(orig_img, p1, p2, Scalar(0, 0, 255));
        imshow(IN_WIN, orig_img); // Show image
    }
    return;
}
```

The callback function declares `static` its local variables, so they maintain their values between calls. The variables, p1 and p2, store the points for defining the rectangular region of interest, and p2set holds the Boolean (`bool`) value that indicates if point p2 is set. When p2set is `true`, a new selected region can be drawn and its new values computed.

The mouse callback function handles the following events:

- EVENT_LBUTTONDOWN: This button is also called left button down. The initial position (p1) is set to `Point(x, y)` where the event occurs. Also, the p2set variable is set to `false`.

- EVENT_MOUSEMOVE && EVENT_FLAG_LBUTTON: Move the mouse with the left button down. First, the boundaries should be checked so that we can correct coordinates and avoid errors just in case the final point is out of the window. Then, the temporal p2 point is set to the final position of the mouse and p2set is set to `true`. Finally, a temporal image is shown in the window with the rectangle drawn on it.

- EVENT_LBUTTONUP: This button is also called left button up and is valid only if p2set is true.The final region is selected. Then a subarray can be pointed in the original image for further computation. After that, a rectangle around the final region is drawn in the original image and the result is shown into the application window.

Next, we take a closer look at the code:

- Size Mat::size() const: Returns the matrix size (Size(cols, rows)): This function is used to get the bounds of the image (orig_img) as follows:

```
if (x > orig_img.size().width) // Check out bounds
        x = orig_img.size().width;
    else if (x < 0)
        x = 0;
    if (y > orig_img.size().height) // Check out bounds
        y = orig_img.size().height;
```

Since Mat::size() returns a Size object, we can access its members width and height to obtain the greatest values for x and y in the image (orig_img) and compare those with the coordinates where the mouse event take place.

- void Mat::copyTo(OutputArray m) const: This method copies the matrix to another one, reallocating new size and type if it is needed. Before copying, the following method invokes:

```
m.create(this->size(), this->type());
```

In the example, the following method is employed to make a temporal copy of the original image:

```
orig_img.copyTo(tmp_img); // Copy orig. to temp. image
```

The rectangle that defines the selected region is drawn over this temporal image.

- `void rectangle(Mat& img, Point pt1, Point pt2, const Scalar& color, int thickness=1, int lineType=8, int shift=0):` This function draws a rectangle defined by points `pt1` and `pt2` over the image (`img`) with the specified `color`, `thickness`, and `lineType`. In the code example, this function is used twice. First, to draw a red (`Scalar(0, 0, 255)`) rectangle on the temporal image (`tmp_img`) around the selected area, and then to draw the boundaries of the final selected region in the original image (`orig_img`):

```
rectangle(tmp_img, p1, p2, Scalar(0, 0 ,255));
//...
rectangle(orig_img, p1, p2, Scalar(0, 0, 255));
```

- `Mat::Mat(const Mat& m, const Rect& roi):` The constructor takes a submatrix of `m` limited by the rectangle (`roi`) that represents a region of interest in the image stored in `m`. This constructor is applied, in the code example, to get the rectangular region whose contrast has to be converted:

```
Mat submat = orig_img(Rect(p1, p2));// Set subarray on
  orig. image
```

Using Qt-based functions

While `highgui` will be sufficient for most purposes, the Qt UI framework (available at http://qt-project.org/) can be leveraged in OpenCV to develop richer user interfaces. A number of OpenCV's user interface functions use the Qt library behind the scenes. In order to use these functions, OpenCV must have been compiled with the `WITH_QT` option.

Note that Qt is a class and **widget** library that allows the creation of full-fledged applications with rich, event-driven user interfaces. In this section, however, we will mainly focus on specific Qt-based functions within OpenCV. Programming with Qt is out of the scope of this book.

With Qt support on, windows created with the `namedWindow` function will automatically look like what is shown in the following screenshot. There is a toolbar with useful functions such as pan, zoom, and save image. Windows also display a status bar at the bottom with the current mouse location and RGB value under that pixel. Right-clicking on the image will display a pop-up menu with the same toolbar options.

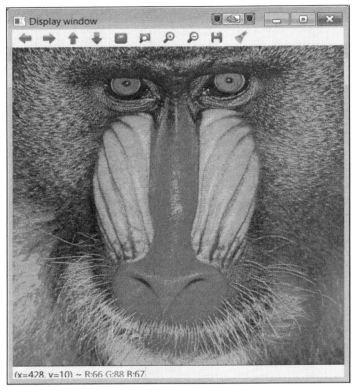

Window displayed with Qt support enabled

Text overlays and status bar

Text can be displayed on a line across the top of the image. This is very useful to show frames per second, number of detections, filenames, and so on. The main function is `displayOverlay(const string& winname, const string& text, int delayms=0)`. The function expects a window identifier and the text to display. Multiple lines are allowed by using the `\n` character in the text string. The text will be displayed in the center and has a fixed size. The `delayms` parameter allows to display the text only for a specified amount of milliseconds (`0=forever`).

We can also display user text in the status bar. This text will replace the default *x* and *y* coordinates and RGB value under the current pixel. The `displayStatusBar(const string& winname, const string& text, int delayms=0)` function has the same parameters as the previous `displayOverlay` function. When the delay has passed, the default status bar text will be displayed.

The properties dialog

One of the most useful features of OpenCV's Qt-based functions is the properties dialog window. This window can be used to place trackbars and buttons. Again, this comes in handy while tuning parameters for our application. The properties dialog window can be accessed by pressing the last button in the toolbar (as shown in the preceding screenshot) or by pressing *Ctrl + P*. The window will only be accessible if trackbars or button have been assigned to it. To create a trackbar for the properties dialog, simply use the `createTrackbar` function passing an empty string (not NULL) as the window name.

Buttons can also be added to the properties dialog. Since both the original window and the dialog windows can be visible at the same time, this can be useful to activate/deactivate features in our application and see the results immediately. To add buttons to the dialog, use the `createButton(const string& button_name, ButtonCallback on_change, void* userdata=NULL, inttype=CV_PUSH_BUTTON, bool initial_button_state=0)` function. The first parameter is the button label (that is, the text to be displayed in the button). Every time the button changes its state, the `on_change` callback function will be called. This should be in the form `void on_change(intstate, void *userdata)`. The userdata pointer passed to `createButton` will be passed to this callback function every time it is called. The state parameter signals the button change and it will have a different value for each type of button, given by parameter types:

- `CV_PUSH_BUTTON`: Push button
- `CV_CHECKBOX`: Checkbox button; the state will be either 1 or 0
- `CV_RADIOBOX`: Radiobox button; the state will be either 1 or 0

For the first two types, the callback is called once on each press. For the radiobox button, it is called both for the button just clicked and for the button that goes unclicked.

Buttons are organized into button bars. Button bars occupy one row in the dialog window. Each new button is added to the right of the last one. Trackbars take up an entire row, so button bars are terminated when a trackbar is added. The following `propertyDlgButtons` example shows how buttons and trackbars are laid out in the properties dialog:

```cpp
#include "opencv2/core/core.hpp"
#include "opencv2/highgui/highgui.hpp"
#include <iostream>

using namespace std;
using namespace cv;

Mat image;
const char win[]="Flip image";

void on_flipV(int state, void *p)
{
    flip(image, image, 0);  // flip vertical
    imshow(win, image);
}

void on_flipH(int state, void *p)
{
    flip(image, image, 1);  // flip horizontal
    imshow(win, image);
}

void on_negative(int state, void *p)
{
    bitwise_not(image, image);  // invert all channels
    imshow(win, image);
}

int main(int argc, char *argv[])
{
    if (argc != 2) {//Check args.
        cout << "Usage: <cmd><file_in>\n";
        return -1;
    }
    image = imread(argv[1]);
    if (image.empty()) {
        cout << "Error! Input image cannot be read...\n";
        return -1;
    }

    namedWindow(win);
    imshow(win, image);
```

```
        displayOverlay(win, argv[1], 0);
        createButton("Flip Vertical", on_flipV, NULL, CV_PUSH_BUTTON);
        createButton("Flip Horizontal", on_flipH, NULL, CV_PUSH_BUTTON);
        int v=0;
        createTrackbar("trackbar1", "", &v, 255);
        createButton("Negative", on_negative, NULL, CV_CHECKBOX);

        cout << "Press any key to exit...\n";
        waitKey();
        return 0;
}
```

This code is similar to the `flipImage` example in the previous chapter. In this example, an image filename is passed as an argument. A properties window is created with two buttons for vertical and horizontal flipping, a dummy trackbar, and a checkbox button to invert color intensities. The callback functions `on_flipV` and `on_flipH` simply flip the current image and show the result (we use a global image variable for this), while the callback function `on_negative` logically inverts color intensities and shows the result. Note that the trackbar is not really being used; it is used to show the **line feed** effect. The following screenshot shows the result:

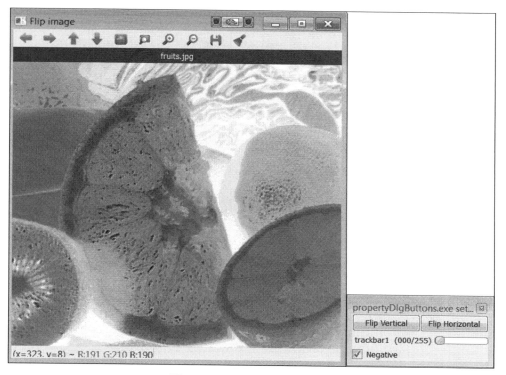

The propertyDlgButtons example

Windows properties

As mentioned previously, by default, all new windows will look like what's shown in the screenshot in the *Using Qt-based functions* section. Still, we can display windows in the non-Qt format by passing the CV_GUI_NORMAL option to namedWindow. On the other hand, window size parameters can be retrieved and set using the double getWindowProperty(const string& winname, int prop_id) and setWindowProperty (const string& winname, int prop_id,double prop_value) functions. The following table shows the properties that can be changed:

Property (prop_id)	Description	Possible values
CV_WND_PROP_FULLSCREEN	Displays a fullscreen or regular window	CV_WINDOW_NORMAL or CV_WINDOW_FULLSCREEN
CV_WND_PROP_AUTOSIZE	Window automatically resizes to fit the displayed image	CV_WINDOW_NORMAL or CV_WINDOW_AUTOSIZE
CV_WND_PROP_ASPECTRATIO	Allows resized windows to have any ratio or fixed original ratio	CV_WINDOW_FREERATIO or CV_WINDOW_KEEPRATIO

More importantly, window properties can be saved. This includes not only size and location, but also flags, trackbar values, zoom, and panning location. To save and load window properties, use the saveWindowParameters(const string& windowName) and loadWindowParameters(const string& windowName) functions.

Qt images

If we want to use the Qt libraries extensively in our project (that is, beyond OpenCV's Qt-based functions), we have to find a way to convert OpenCV's images to the format used by Qt (QImage). This can be done by using the following function:

```
QImage* Mat2Qt(const Mat &image)
{
Mat temp=image.clone();
cvtColor(image, temp, CV_BGR2RGB);
QImage *imgQt= new QImage((const unsigned
  char*)(temp.data),temp.cols,temp.rows,QImage::Format_RGB888);
return imgQt;
}
```

This function creates a Qt image using OpenCV's image data. Note that a conversion is first necessary, since Qt uses RGB images while OpenCV uses BGR order.

Finally, to display the image with Qt, we have at least two options:

- Create a class that extends the `QWidget` class and implements paint events.
- Create a label and set it to draw an image (using the `setPixMap` method).

Summary

In this chapter, we provided a deeper view of the `highgui` module functionality to enrich the user experience. The main elements supplied by OpenCV to build graphical user interfaces are shown in some code samples. Moreover, we reviewed the new Qt functionality inside OpenCV.

The chapter's examples cover topics such as `tbarContrast`, `tbarContrastCallB`, `drawThings`, `drawRs`, and `propertyDlgButtons`.

The next chapter will cover the implementation of the most usual methods used for image processing, such as brightness control, contrast and color conversion, retina filtering, and geometrical transformations.

First Things First – Image Processing

3

Image processing refers to digital processing of any two-dimensional data (a picture) by a computer by applying signal processing methods. Image processing has a broad spectrum of applications, such as image representation, image enhancement or sharpening, image restoration by means of filtering, and geometrical correction. These applications are usually the first stage and input to the following stages in a computer vision system. In OpenCV, there is a specific module, `imgproc`, for image processing. In this chapter, we will cover the most important and frequently used methods available in the library, that is, pixel-level access, histogram manipulation, image equalization, brightness and contracts modeling, color spaces, filtering, and arithmetic and geometrical transforms.

Pixel-level access and common operations

One of the most fundamental operations in image processing is pixel-level access. Since an image is contained in the `Mat` matrix type, there is a generic access form that uses the `at<>` template function. In order to use it, we have to specify the type of matrix cells, for example:

```
Mat src1 = imread("stuff.jpg", CV_LOAD_IMAGE_GRAYSCALE);
uchar pixel1=src1.at<uchar>(0,0);
cout << "First pixel: " << (unsigned int)pixel1 << endl;
Mat src2 = imread("stuff.jpg", CV_LOAD_IMAGE_COLOR);
Vec3b pixel2 = src2.at<Vec3b>(0,0);
cout << "First pixel (B):" << (unsigned int)pixel2[0] << endl;
cout << "First pixel (G):" << (unsigned int)pixel2[1] << endl;
cout << "First pixel (R):" << (unsigned int)pixel2[2] << endl;
```

Note that color images use the `Vec3b` type, which is an array of three unsigned chars. Images with a fourth alpha (transparency) channel would be accessed using the type `Vec4b`. The `Scalar` type represents a 1 to 4-element vector and can also be used in all these cases. Note that `at<>` can be also used to change pixel values (that is, on the left-hand side of an assignment).

Apart from pixel access, there are a number of common operations for which we should know the corresponding snippets. The following table shows these common operations:

Operation	Code example

Obtain size of matrix	`Size siz=src.size();`
	`cout << "width: " << siz.width << endl;`
	`cout << "height: " << siz.height << endl;`

Obtain number of channels	`int nc=src.channels();`
Obtain pixel data type	`int d=src.depth();`

Set matrix values	`src.setTo(0); //for one-channel src`
	Or
	`src.setTo(Scalar(b,g,r)); // for three-channel src`

Create a copy of the matrix	`Mat dst=src.clone();`
Create a copy of the matrix (with optional mask)	`src.copy(dst, mask);`
Reference a submatrix	`Mat dst=src(Range(r1,r2),Range(c1,c2));`
Create a new matrix from a submatrix (that is, image crop)	`Rect roi(r1,c2, width, height);` `Mat dst=src(roi).clone();`

Note the difference in the last two rows: in the last row, a new matrix is created. The case of the penultimate row only creates a reference to a submatrix within `src`, but data is not actually copied.

> The most common operations, including additional iterator-based pixel access methods, are summarized in the *OpenCV 2.4 Cheat Sheet*, which can be downloaded from `http://docs.opencv.org/trunk/opencv_cheatsheet.pdf`.

Image histogram

An image histogram represents the frequency of the occurrence of the various gray levels or colors in the image, in case of 2D and 3D histograms respectively. Therefore, the histogram is similar to the probability density function of the different pixel values, that is, the gray levels, present in the image. In OpenCV, the image histogram may be calculated with the function `void calcHist(const Mat* images, int nimages, const int* channels, InputArray mask, OutputArray hist, int dims, const int* histSize, const float** ranges, bool uniform=true, bool accumulate=false)`. The first parameter is a pointer to the input image. It is possible to calculate the histogram of more than one input image. This allows you to compare image histograms and calculate the joint histogram of several images. The second parameter is the number of source images. The third input parameter is the list of the channels used to compute the histogram. It is possible to calculate the histogram of more than one channel of the same color image. Thus, in this case, the `nimages` value will be 1 and the `const int* channels` parameter will be an array with the list of channel numbers.

The number of channels goes from zero to two. The parameter `InputArray mask` is an optional mask to indicate the array elements (image pixels) counted in the histogram. The fifth parameter is the output histogram. The parameter `int dims` is the histogram dimensionality that must be positive and not greater than 32 (`CV_MAX_DIMS`). A histogram can be n-dimensional according to the number of bins used to quantize the pixel values of the image. The parameter `const int* histSize` is the array of histogram sizes in each dimension. It allows us to compute histograms with non-uniform binning (or quantification). The `const float** ranges` parameter is the array of the `dims` arrays of the histogram bin boundaries in each dimension. The last two parameters have Boolean values and by default are `true` and `false` respectively. They indicate that the histogram is uniform and non-accumulative.

The following `ImgHisto` example shows how to calculate and display the one-dimensional histogram of a 2D image:

```
#include "opencv2/imgproc/imgproc.hpp" // a dedicated include file
#include "opencv2/highgui/highgui.hpp"
#include <iostream>

using namespace cv;
using namespace std;

int main( int argc, char *argv[])
```

```
{
    int histSize = 255;

    long int dim;
    Mat hist, image;

    //Read original image
    Mat src = imread( "fruits.jpg");

    //Convert color image to gray level image
    cvtColor(src, image, CV_RGB2GRAY);

    //Create three windows
    namedWindow("Source", 0);
    namedWindow("Gray Level Image", 0);
    namedWindow("Histogram", WINDOW_AUTOSIZE);

    imshow("Source", src);
    imshow("Gray Level Image", image);

    calcHist(&image, 1, 0, Mat(), hist, 1, &histSize, 0);

    dim=image.rows *image.cols;
    Mat histImage = Mat::ones(255, 255, CV_8U)*255;

    normalize(hist, hist, 0, histImage.rows, CV_MINMAX, CV_32F);

    histImage = Scalar::all(255);
    int binW = cvRound((double)histImage.cols/histSize);

    for( int i = 0; i < histSize; i++ )
    rectangle( histImage, Point(i*binW, histImage.rows),
        Point((i+1)*binW, histImage.rows -
            cvRound(hist.at<float>(i))), Scalar::all(0), -1, 8, 0
                );
    imshow("Histogram", histImage);

    cout << "Press any key to exit...\n";
    waitKey(); // Wait for key press
    return 0;
}
```

The code explanation is given here: the example creates three windows with the source image, the grayscale image, and the result of the 1D histogram. The 1D histogram is shown as a bar diagram for the 255 gray values. Thus, first the color pixels are converted into gray values using the `cvtColor` function. The gray values are then normalized using the `normalize` function between 0 and the maximum gray level value. Then the 1D histogram is calculated by discretizing the colors in the image into a number of bins and counting the number of image pixels in each bin. The following screenshot shows the output of the example. Note that a new include file, `imgproc.hpp`, dedicated to image processing is needed.

Output of the histogram example

Histogram equalization

Once the image histogram is calculated, it can be modelled so that the image is modified and the histogram has a different shape. This is useful to change the low-contrast levels of images with narrow histograms, since this will spread out the gray levels and thus enhance the contrast. Histogram modeling, also known as histogram transfer, is a powerful technique for image enhancement. In histogram equalization, the goal is to obtain a uniform histogram for the output image. That is, a flat histogram where each pixel value has the same probability. In OpenCV, histogram equalization is performed with the function `void equalizeHist(InputArray src, OutputArray dst)`. The first parameter is the input image and the second one is the output image with the histogram equalized.

The following `EqualizeHist_Demo` example shows how to calculate and display the histogram equalized and the effect on the two-dimensional image:

```
#include "opencv2/highgui/highgui.hpp"
#include "opencv2/imgproc/imgproc.hpp"
#include <iostream>
```

```
#include <stdio.h>

using namespace cv;
using namespace std;

int main( int, char *argv[] )
{
  Mat src, image, hist;
  int histSize = 255;
  long int dim;

  //Read original image
  src = imread( "fruits.jpg");

  //Convert to grayscale
  cvtColor( src, src, COLOR_BGR2GRAY );

  //Apply Histogram Equalization
  equalizeHist( src, image );

  //Display results
  namedWindow("Source image", 0 );
  namedWindow("Equalized Image", 0 );

  imshow( "Source image", src );
  imshow( "Equalized Image", image );

  //Calculate Histogram of the Equalized Image and display
  calcHist(&image, 1, 0, Mat(), hist, 1, &histSize, 0);
  dim=image.rows *image.cols;
  Mat histImage = Mat::ones(255, 255, CV_8U)*255;
  normalize(hist, hist, 0, histImage.rows, CV_MINMAX, CV_32F);
  histImage = Scalar::all(255);
  int binW = cvRound((double)histImage.cols/histSize);

  for( int i = 0; i < histSize; i++ )
  rectangle( histImage, Point(i*binW, histImage.rows),
    Point((i+1)*binW, histImage.rows -
      cvRound(hist.at<float>(i))), Scalar::all(0), -1, 8, 0 );

  namedWindow("Histogram Equalized Image", WINDOW_AUTOSIZE);
  imshow("Histogram Equalized Image", histImage);

  waitKey();// Exits the program
  return 0;
}
```

The code explanation is given as follows. The example first reads the original image and converts it to grayscale. Then, histogram equalization is performed using the `equalizeHist` function. Finally, the histogram of the equalized image is shown together with the two previous images. The following screenshot shows the output of the example, where three windows are created with the grayscale image, the equalized image, and its histogram:

Output of the histogram equalization example

Brightness and contrast modeling

The brightness of an object is the perceived luminance or intensity and depends on the luminance of the environment. Two objects in different environments could have the same luminance but different brightness. The reason is that the human visual perception is sensitive to luminance contrast rather than absolute luminance. Contrast is the difference in luminance and/or color that makes an object distinguishable compared to other objects within the same field of view. The maximum contrast of an image is known as the contrast ratio or dynamic range.

It is possible to modify the brightness and contrast of an image by means of point-wise operations. Point operations map a given gray pixel value into a different gray level according to a transform previously defined. In OpenCV, point operations may be performed with the function `void Mat::convertTo(OutputArray m, int rtype, double alpha=1, double beta=0)`. The `convertTo` function converts an image array to another data type with optional scaling. The first parameter is the output image and the second parameter is the output matrix type, that is, the depth, since the number of channels is the same as the input image. Thus, the source pixel values `I(x,y)` are converted to the target data type with the new value `(I(x,y) * alpha + beta)`.

The following `BrightnessContrast` example shows how to perform an image pixel (point) operation to modify brightness and contrast:

```cpp
#include "opencv2/imgproc/imgproc.hpp"
#include "opencv2/highgui/highgui.hpp"

#include <iostream>

using namespace cv;
using namespace std;

int init_brightness  = 100;
int init_contrast = 100;

Mat image;

/* brightness and contrast function to highlight the image*/
void updateBrightnessContrast(int, void* )
{
    int histSize = 255;
    int var_brightness = init_brightness  - 100;
    int var_contrast = init_contrast - 100;

    double a, b;
    if( var_contrast > 0 )
    {
        double delta = 127.*var_contrast/100;
        a = 255./(255. - delta*2);
        b = a*(var_brightness - delta);
    }
    else
    {
        double delta = -128.*var_contrast/100;
        a = (256.-delta*2)/255.;
        b = a*var_brightness + delta;
    }

    Mat dst, hist;

    image.convertTo(dst, CV_8U, a, b);

    imshow("image", dst);

    calcHist(&dst, 1, 0, Mat(), hist, 1, &histSize, 0);
```

```
    Mat histImage = Mat::ones(200, 320, CV_8U)*255;

    normalize(hist, hist, 0, histImage.rows, CV_MINMAX, CV_32F);

    histImage = Scalar::all(255);
    int binW = cvRound((double)histImage.cols/histSize);

    for( int i = 0; i < histSize; i++ )
        rectangle( histImage, Point(i*binW, histImage.rows),
            Point((i+1)*binW, histImage.rows -
                cvRound(hist.at<float>(i))), Scalar::all(0), -1,
                    8, 0 );
        imshow("histogram", histImage);
    }

const char* keys = {
    "{1| |fruits.jpg|input image file}"
};

int main( int argc, const char** argv )
    {
        CommandLineParser parser(argc, argv, keys);
        string inputImage = parser.get<string>("1");

        //Read the input image.
        image = imread( inputImage, 0 );
        namedWindow("image", 0);
        namedWindow("histogram", 0);

        createTrackbar("brightness", "image", &init_brightness ,
            200, updateBrightnessContrast);
        createTrackbar("contrast", "image", &init_contrast, 200,
            updateBrightnessContrast);

        updateBrightnessContrast(0, 0);

    waitKey();
    return 0;
}
```

The code explanation is given here: the example creates two windows with the grayscale image and its histogram. The new values for the brightness and contrast are selected by the user using the function `createTrackbar`. This function attaches two sliders or range controls to the image for brightness and contrast. The following screenshot shows the output of the `BrightnessContrast` example for a value of 148 for brightness and 81 for contrast:

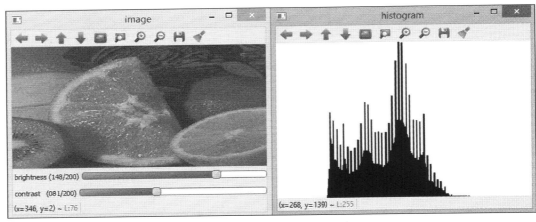

Output of the brightness and contrast image modification

Histogram matching and LUT

The histogram may also be used to modify the color of an image. Histogram matching is a method of color adjustment between two color images. Given a reference image and a target image, the result (destination image) will be equal to the target image except that its (three) histograms will look like those of the reference image. This effect is known as **color mapping** or **color transfer**.

The histogram matching algorithm is run over each of the three color histograms independently. For each channel, the **cumulative distribution function (cdf)** has to be calculated. For a given channel, let `Fr` be the cdf of the reference image and `Ft` be the cdf of the target image. Then, for each pixel `v` in the reference image, we find the gray level `w`, for which `Fr(v)=Ft(w)`. The pixel with value `v` is thus changed to `w`.

Next, we provide another example of histograms in which we use a technique called histogram matching. The example also uses **look-up tables** (LUT). A look-up table transformation assigns a new pixel value to each pixel in the input image (there is a good explanation and example of an LUT at http://docs.opencv. org/doc/tutorials/core/how_to_scan_images/how_to_scan_images.html). The new values are given by a table. Thus, the first entry in this table gives the new value for pixel value 0, the second the new value for pixel value 1, and so on. Assuming we use a source and destination image, the transform is then given by Dst(x,y)=LUT(Src(x,y)).

The OpenCV function for performing a look-up table transformation is LUT(InputArray src, InputArray lut, OutputArray dst, int interpolation=0). The parameter src is an 8-bit image. The table is given in the parameter lut, which has 256 elements. The table has either one channel or the same number of channels as the source image.

The following is the histMatching example:

```
#include "opencv2/opencv.hpp"
#include <iostream>

using namespace std;
using namespace cv;

void histMatch(const Mat &reference, const Mat &target, Mat
    &result){
    float const HISTMATCH = 0.000001;
    double min, max;

    vector<Mat> ref_channels;
    split(reference, ref_channels);
    vector<Mat> tgt_channels;
    split(target, tgt_channels);

    int histSize = 256;
    float range[] = {0, 256};
    const float* histRange = { range };
    bool uniform = true;

    //For every channel (B, G, R)
    for ( int i=0 ; i<3 ; i++ )
    {
        Mat ref_hist, tgt_hist;
```

```
Mat ref_hist_accum, tgt_hist_accum;

//Calculate histograms
calcHist(&ref_channels[i], 1, 0, Mat(), ref_hist, 1,
    &histSize, &histRange, uniform, false);
calcHist(&tgt_channels[i], 1, 0, Mat(), tgt_hist, 1,
    &histSize, &histRange, uniform, false);

//Normalize histograms
minMaxLoc(ref_hist, &min, &max);
if (max==0) continue;
ref_hist = ref_hist / max;
minMaxLoc(tgt_hist, &min, &max);
if (max==0) continue;
tgt_hist = tgt_hist / max;

//Calculate accumulated histograms
ref_hist.copyTo(ref_hist_accum);
tgt_hist.copyTo(tgt_hist_accum);

float * src_cdf_data = ref_hist_accum.ptr<float>();
float * dst_cdf_data = tgt_hist_accum.ptr<float>();

for ( int j=1 ; j < 256 ; j++ )
{
    src_cdf_data[j] = src_cdf_data[j] + src_cdf_data[j-1];
    dst_cdf_data[j] = dst_cdf_data[j] + dst_cdf_data[j-1];
}
//Normalize accumulated
minMaxLoc(ref_hist_accum, &min, &max);
ref_hist_accum = ref_hist_accum / max;
minMaxLoc(tgt_hist_accum, &min, &max);
tgt_hist_accum = tgt_hist_accum / max;

//Result max
Mat Mv(1, 256, CV_8UC1);
uchar * M = Mv.ptr<uchar>();
uchar last = 0;
for ( int j=0 ; j < tgt_hist_accum.rows ; j++ )
{
    float F1 = dst_cdf_data[j];

    for ( uchar k=last ; k < ref_hist_accum.rows ; k++ )
```

```
        {
            float F2 = src_cdf_data[k];
            if ( std::abs(F2 - F1) < HISTMATCH ||  F2 > F1 )
            {
                M[j] = k;
                last = k;
                break;
            }
        }
    }
}
Mat lut(1, 256, CV_8UC1, M);
LUT(tgt_channels[i], lut, tgt_channels[i]);
    }

    //Merge the three channels into the result image
    merge(tgt_channels, result);
}

int main(int argc, char *argv[])
{
    //Read original image and clone it to contain results
    Mat ref = imread("baboon.jpg", CV_LOAD_IMAGE_COLOR );
    Mat tgt = imread("lena.jpg", CV_LOAD_IMAGE_COLOR );
    Mat dst = tgt.clone();

    //Create three windows
    namedWindow("Reference", WINDOW_AUTOSIZE);
    namedWindow("Target", WINDOW_AUTOSIZE);
    namedWindow("Result", WINDOW_AUTOSIZE);
    imshow("Reference", ref);
    imshow("Target", tgt);

    histMatch(ref, tgt, dst);
    imshow("Result", dst);

    // Position windows on screen
    moveWindow("Reference", 0,0);
    moveWindow("Target", ref.cols,0);
    moveWindow("Result", ref.cols+tgt.cols,0);

    waitKey(); // Wait for key press
    return 0;
}
```

The code explanation is given here: the example first reads the reference and target images. The output image is also allocated. The main function is `histMatch`. In it, the reference and target images are first split into the three color channels. Then, for every channel, we obtain the normalized histograms of reference and target images, followed by the respective cdfs. Next, the histogram matching transformation is performed.

Finally, we apply the new pixel values using the look-up table. Note that the transformation could also be applied by iterating over every pixel in the result image. The look-up table option is, however, much faster. The following screenshot shows the output of the sample. The color palette of the reference image (the `baboon.jpg` image) is transferred to the target image.

Output of the histMatching example

Conversion from RGB to other color spaces

The color of an image may also be modified by changing the color space. In OpenCV, six color models are available and it is possible to convert from one to another by using the `cvtColor` function.

 The default color format in OpenCV is often referred to as RGB but it is actually BGR (the channels are reversed).

The function `void cvtColor(InputArray src, OutputArray dst, int code, int dstCn=0)` has the input and output images as the first and second parameters. The third parameter is the color space conversion code and the last parameter is the number of channels in the output image; if this parameter is 0, the number of channels is obtained automatically from the input image.

The following `color_channels` example shows how to convert from RGB to HSV, Luv, Lab, YCrCb, and XYZ color spaces:

```cpp
#include "opencv2/highgui/highgui.hpp"
#include "opencv2/imgproc/imgproc.hpp"

using namespace cv;
using namespace std;

int main( ){
    Mat image, HSV, Luv, Lab, YCrCb, XYZ;

    //Read image
    image = imread("HappyFish.jpg", CV_LOAD_IMAGE_COLOR);

    //Convert RGB image to different color spaces
    cvtColor(image, HSV, CV_RGB2HSV);
    cvtColor(image, Luv, CV_RGB2Luv);
    cvtColor(image, Lab, CV_RGB2Lab);
    cvtColor(image, YCrCb, CV_RGB2YCrCb);
    cvtColor(image, XYZ, CV_RGB2XYZ);

    //Create windows and display results
    namedWindow( "Source Image", 0 );
    namedWindow( "Result HSV Image", 0 );
    namedWindow( "Result Luv Image", 0 );
    namedWindow( "Result Lab Image", 0 );
    namedWindow( "Result YCrCb Image", 0 );
    namedWindow( "Result XYZ Image", 0 );

    imshow( "Source Image", image );
    imshow( "Result HSV Image",  HSV );
    imshow( "Result Luv Image", Luv );
    imshow( "Result Lab Image", Lab);
    imshow( "Result YCrCb Image", YCrCb );
    imshow( "Result XYZ Image", XYZ );

    waitKey(); //Wait for key press
    return 0;  //End the program
}
```

The code explanation is given here: the first example reads the original image and makes the conversion into five different color models. The original image in RGB and the results are then displayed. The following screenshot shows the output of the sample:

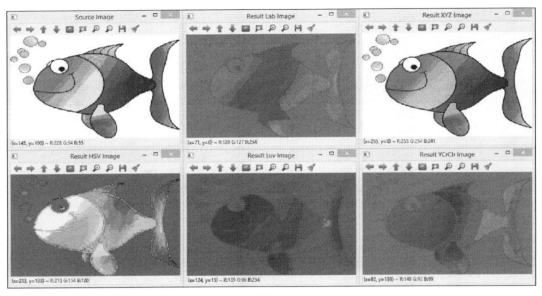

Output of the different color spaces

Filtering with the retina model

Image restoration is concerned with filtering the digital image to minimize the effect of degradations. Degradation is produced by the sensing environment during image acquisition by optical or electronic devices. The effectiveness of image filtering depends on the extent and the accuracy of the knowledge of the degradation process as well as on the filter design.

In OpenCV, there are several isotropic and anisotropic filters available operating on both spatial and frequency domains. One of the most recent filters is the retina filter, which is based on a model of the human visual system. There is a class named `Retina` to perform spatio-temporal filtering modeling the two main retina information channels, which are **parvocellular** (`parvo`) due to foveal vision and **magnocellular** (`magno`) due to peripheral vision. The `parvo` channel is related to detail extraction while the `magno` channel is dedicated to motion analysis.

The `Retina` class may be applied on still images, images sequences, and video sequences to perform motion analysis. Here we present a simplified version of the `retinademo` algorithm provided in OpenCV. The algorithm `Filter_Retina.cpp` presented here demonstrates the use of the retina model images, which can be used to perform texture analysis with enhanced signal-to-noise ratio and enhanced details that are robust against input image luminance ranges. The main properties of the human retina model are as follows:

- Spectral whitening (mid-frequency detail enhancement)

- High-frequency spatio-temporal noise reduction (temporal noise and high-frequency spatial noise are minimized)

- Low-frequency luminance reduction (luminance range compression): High-luminance regions do not hide details in darker regions anymore

- Local logarithmic luminance compression allows details to be enhanced even in low-light conditions

 For more information, refer to *Using Human Visual System Modeling for bio-inspired low level image processing, Benoit A., Caplier A., Durette B., Herault J.,* Elsevier, Computer Vision and Image Understanding 114 (2010), pp. 758-773. DOI at `http://dx.doi.org/10.1016/j.cviu.2010.01.011`.

The following is the code for the example:

```cpp
#include "opencv2/opencv.hpp"
using namespace cv;
using namespace std;
int main(int argc, char* argv[])
{
    //Declare input image and retina output buffers
    Mat src, retinaOutput_parvo, retinaOutput_magno;

    src = imread("starry_night.jpg", 1); // load image in RGB

    //Create a retina instance with default parameters setup
    Ptr< Retina> myRetina;

    //Allocate "classical" retina :
    myRetina = new  Retina(src.size());

    //Save default retina parameters file
    myRetina->write("RetinaDefaultParameters.xml");

    //The retina parameters may be reload using method "setup"
```

```
                    //Uncomment to load parameters if file exists
                    //myRetina->setup("RetinaSpecificParameters.xml");
                    myRetina->clearBuffers();

                    //Several iteration of the filter may be done
                    for( int iter = 1; iter < 6; iter++ ){
                        // run retina filter
                        myRetina->run(src);

                        // Retrieve and display retina output
                        myRetina->getParvo(retinaOutput_parvo);
                        myRetina->getMagno(retinaOutput_magno);

                        //Create windows and display results
                        namedWindow("Source Image", 0 );
                        namedWindow("Retina Parvo", 0 );
                        namedWindow("Retina Magno", 0 );

                        imshow("Source Image", src);
                        imshow("Retina Parvo", retinaOutput_parvo);
                        imshow("Retina Magno", retinaOutput_magno);
                    }
                    cout<<"Retina demo end"<< endl;    // Program end message
                    waitKey();
                    return 0;
                }
```

The code explanation is given here: the example first reads the input image and obtains the retina model of the image using classical parameters for the model. The retina can be settled up with various parameters; by default, the retina cancels mean luminance and enforces all details of the visual scene. The filter is then run five times and the `parvo` and `magno` images and its details are shown. The following screenshot shows the output of the retina model filter after the five iterations:

Output of the retina filter after five iterations

Arithmetic and geometrical transforms

An arithmetic transform changes the value of an image pixel and it is applied point to point, whereas a geometrical transform changes the position of the image pixels. Thus, points in an image get a new position in the output image without changing their intensity values. Examples of arithmetic transforms may be addition, subtraction, and division between images. Examples of geometrical transforms are scaling, translation, and rotation of images. More complex transformations are to solve the barrel and cushion deformations of an image produced by an optical lens.

In OpenCV, there are several functions to perform arithmetic and geometrical transforms. Here we show two examples for image addition and perspective transformation by means of the functions `addWeighted` and `warpPerspective` respectively.

Arithmetic transform

The function `addWeighted` performs a linear combination of two images, that is, addition of two weighted images to carry out a linear blending. The function `void addWeighted(InputArray src1, double alpha, InputArray src2, double beta, double gamma, OutputArray dst, int dtype=-1)` has two input images as the first and third parameters with their weights (second and fourth parameter). Then, the output image is the sixth parameter. The fifth parameter, `gamma`, is a scalar added to each sum. The last parameter `dtype` is optional and refers to the depth of the output image; when both input images have the same depth, it can be set to `-1`.

The following `LinearBlend` example shows how to perform a linear blending between two images:

```cpp
#include "opencv2/highgui/highgui.hpp"

using namespace cv;
using namespace std;

int main()
{
    double alpha = 0.5, beta, input;
    Mat src1, src2, dst;

    //Read images (same size and type )
    src1 = imread("baboon.jpg");
```

```
src2 = imread("lena.jpg");
 //Create windows
namedWindow("Final Linear Blend", CV_WINDOW_AUTOSIZE );

//Perform a loop with 101 iteration for linear blending
for(int k = 0; k <= 100; ++k ){
    alpha = (double)k/100;
    beta  = 1 - alpha;

    addWeighted( src2, alpha, src1, beta, 0.0, dst );

    imshow( "Final Linear Blend", dst );
    cvWaitKey(50);
}
namedWindow("Original Image 1", CV_WINDOW_AUTOSIZE );
namedWindow("Original Image 2", CV_WINDOW_AUTOSIZE );
imshow( "Original Image 1", src1 );
imshow( "Original Image 2", src2 );

cvWaitKey(); // Wait for key press
return 0;    // End
}
```

The code explanation is given here: the example first reads two images, src1= baboon.jpg and src2= lena.jpg, and then performs a total of 101 linear combinations with different values of the weights alpha and beta. The first linear combination or blend is with alpha equal to zero, and therefore it is the src1 image. The value of alpha increases in the loop while the value of beta decreases. Therefore, the src2 image is combined and superimposed onto the src1 image. This produces a morphing effect and the baboon.jpg image gradually changes into a different image, that is, into lena.jpg. The following screenshot shows the output of several linear blending steps at iterations 1, 10, 20, 30, 40, 50, 70, 85, and 100:

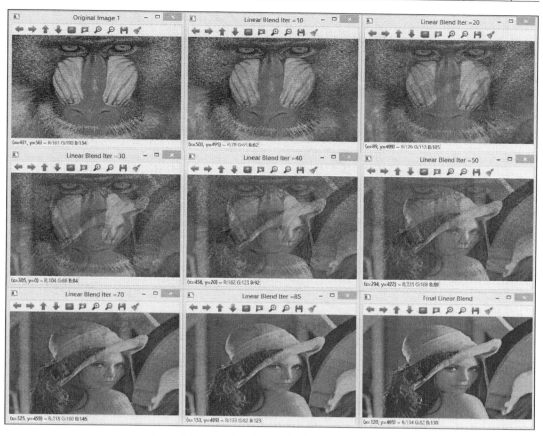

Output of different lineal blending between two images

Geometrical transforms

The function `warpPerspective`, `void ocl::warpPerspective(const oclMat& src, oclMat& dst, const Mat& M, Size dsize, int flags=INTER_LINEAR)` performs a perspective transformation on an image. It has the input or source image `src` as the first parameter and the output or destination image `dst` as the second parameter. Then, the third parameter is a 2 x 3 transformation matrix obtained from the `getPerspectiveTransform` function, which calculates a perspective transform from the positions of four points in the two images in four pairs of corresponding points. The fourth parameter of `warpPerspective` is the size of the output image and the last parameter is the interpolation method. By default, the interpolation method is linear, `INTER_LINEAR`; other methods supported are nearest neighbor `INTER_NEAREST` and cubic `INTER_CUBIC`.

The following `Geometrical_Transform` example performs a perspective transformation to the input image `img.jpg`.

 For full details of the example, refer to *N. Amin, Automatic perspective correction for quadrilateral objects,* at `https://opencv-code.com/tutorials/automatic-perspective-correction-for-quadrilateral-objects/`.

```cpp
#include "opencv2/highgui/highgui.hpp"
#include "opencv2/imgproc/imgproc.hpp"
#include <iostream>
#include <stdio.h>

using namespace cv;
using namespace std;

Point2f centerpoint(0,0);

Point2f computeIntersect(Vec4i a,Vec4i b){
    int x1 = a[0], y1 = a[1], x2 = a[2], y2 = a[3], x3 = b[0], y3
        = b[1], x4 = b[2], y4 = b[3];

    if (float d = ((float)(x1 - x2) * (y3 - y4)) - ((y1 - y2) *
        (x3 - x4)))
    {
        Point2f pnt;
        pnt.x = ((x1 * y2 - y1 * x2) * (x3 - x4) - (x1 - x2) * (x3
            * y4 - y3 * x4)) / d;
        pnt.y = ((x1 * y2 - y1 * x2) * (y3 - y4) - (y1 - y2) * (x3
            * y4 - y3 * x4)) / d;
        return pnt;
    }
    else
    return Point2f(-1, -1);
}

void sortCorners(vector<Point2f>& corner_points, Point2f
    centerpoint)
{
    vector<Point2f> top, bot;

    for (int i = 0; i < corner_points.size(); i++)
    {
        if (corner_points[i].y < centerpoint.y)
        top.push_back(corner_points[i]);
```

```
            else
                bot.push_back(corner_points[i]);
    }

    Point2f tl = top[0].x > top[1].x ? top[1] : top[0];
    Point2f tr = top[0].x > top[1].x ? top[0] : top[1];
    Point2f bl = bot[0].x > bot[1].x ? bot[1] : bot[0];
    Point2f br = bot[0].x > bot[1].x ? bot[0] : bot[1];

    corner_points.clear();
    corner_points.push_back(tl);
    corner_points.push_back(tr);
    corner_points.push_back(br);
    corner_points.push_back(bl);
}

int main(){
    Mat src = imread("img.jpg");
    if (src.empty())
    return -1;

    Mat dst = src.clone();

    Mat bw;
    cvtColor(src, bw, CV_BGR2GRAY);

    Canny(bw, bw, 100, 100, 3);
    vector<Vec4i> lines;
    HoughLinesP(bw, lines, 1, CV_PI/180, 70, 30, 10);

    vector<Point2f> corner_points;
    for (int i = 0; i < lines.size(); i++)
    {
        for (int j = i+1; j < lines.size(); j++)
        {
            Point2f pnt = computeIntersect(lines[i], lines[j]);
            if (pnt.x >= 0 && pnt.y >= 0)
            corner_points.push_back(pnt);
        }
    }

    vector<Point2f> approx;
    approxPolyDP(Mat(corner_points), approx,
        arcLength(Mat(corner_points), true) * 0.02, true);

    if (approx.size() != 4)
```

```
{
    cout << "The object is not quadrilateral!" << endl;
    return -1;
}

//Get center point
for (int i = 0; i < corner_points.size(); i++)
centerpoint += corner_points[i];
centerpoint *= (1. / corner_points.size());

sortCorners(corner_points, centerpoint);

//Draw lines
for (int i = 0; i < lines.size(); i++)
{
    Vec4i v = lines[i];
    line(dst, Point(v[0], v[1]), Point(v[2], v[3]),
        CV_RGB(0,255,0));
}

//Draw corner points
circle(dst, corner_points[0], 3, CV_RGB(255,0,0), 2);
circle(dst, corner_points[1], 3, CV_RGB(0,255,0), 2);
circle(dst, corner_points[2], 3, CV_RGB(0,0,255), 2);
circle(dst, corner_points[3], 3, CV_RGB(255,255,255), 2);

//Draw mass center points
circle(dst, centerpoint, 3, CV_RGB(255,255,0), 2);

//Calculate corresponding points for corner points
Mat quad = Mat::zeros(src.rows, src.cols/2, CV_8UC3);

vector<Point2f> quad_pnts;
quad_pnts.push_back(Point2f(0, 0));
quad_pnts.push_back(Point2f(quad.cols, 0));
quad_pnts.push_back(Point2f(quad.cols, quad.rows));
quad_pnts.push_back(Point2f(0, quad.rows));

// Draw corresponding points
circle(dst, quad_pnts[0], 3, CV_RGB(255,0,0), 2);
circle(dst, quad_pnts[1], 3, CV_RGB(0,255,0), 2);
circle(dst, quad_pnts[2], 3, CV_RGB(0,0,255), 2);
```

```
    circle(dst, quad_pnts[3], 3, CV_RGB(255,255,255), 2);

    Mat transmtx = getPerspectiveTransform(corner_points, quad_pnts);
    warpPerspective(src, quad, transmtx, quad.size());

    //Create windows and display results
    namedWindow("Original Image", CV_WINDOW_AUTOSIZE );
    namedWindow("Selected Points", CV_WINDOW_AUTOSIZE );
    namedWindow("Corrected Perspertive", CV_WINDOW_AUTOSIZE );

    imshow("Original Image", src);
    imshow("Selected Points", dst);
    imshow("Corrected Perspertive", quad);

    waitKey(); //Wait for key press
    return 0;   //End
}
```

The code explanation is given here: the example first reads the input image (`img.jpg`) and calculates the key points of the region of interest or object to perform the perspective transformation. The key points are the corner points of the object. The algorithm only works for quadrilateral objects. The methods to calculate corners (Canny operator and Hough transforms) are explained in *Chapter 4, What's in the Image, Segmentation*. The points corresponding to the object corners are the corners of the output image. These points are shown with circles on the original image. The dimension of the output image is set to the same height and half the width of the input image. Finally, the image with the corrected object is visualized. The perspective correction uses a linear transform, INTER_LINEAR. The following screenshot shows the output of the algorithm:

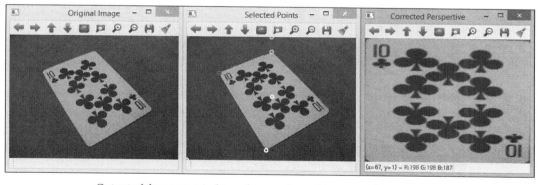

Output of the geometrical transform performed to correct the perspective

Summary

This chapter has covered the most common image processing methods used in computer vision. Image processing is often the step performed just before further computer vision applications. It has many methods and is usually applied for image corrections and enhancement such as image histograms, image equalization, brightness and contrast modeling, image color conversion by means of histogram matching and color space transformations, filtering using the model of the human retina, and arithmetic and geometrical transforms.

The next chapter will cover the next stage in a computer vision system, that is, the segmentation process. We will see how to extract regions of interest within an image.

What else?

Other important functions in OpenCV for image processing are related to filtering. These functions have been omitted in the chapter since they are straightforward. OpenCV includes an example that shows how to use the main filters (`[opencv_source_code]/samples/cpp/filter2D_demo.cpp`). The main filter functions are:

- `GaussianBlur` for a Gaussian filter
- `medianBlur` for a median filter
- `bilateralFilter` for anisotropic filtering
- `blur` for a homogeneous blur

4
What's in the Image? Segmentation

Segmentation is any process that partitions an image into multiple regions or segments. These will typically correspond to meaningful regions or objects, such as face, car, road, sky, grass, and so on. Segmentation is one of the most important stages in a computer vision system. In OpenCV, there is no specific module for segmentation, though a number of ready-to-use methods are available in other modules (most of them in `imgproc`). In this chapter, we will cover the most important and frequently used methods available in the library. In some cases, additional processing will have to be added to improve the results or obtain seeds (this refers to rough segments that allow an algorithm to perform a complete segmentation). In this chapter we will look at the following major segmentation methods: thresholding, contours and connected components, flood filling, watershed segmentation, and the GrabCut algorithm.

Thresholding

Thresholding is one of the simplest yet most useful segmentation operations. We can safely say that you will end up using some sort of thresholding in almost any image-processing application. We consider it a segmentation operation since it partitions an image into two regions, typically, an object and its background. In OpenCV, thresholding is performed with the function `double threshold(InputArray src, OutputArray dst, double thresh, double maxval, int type)`.

The first two parameters are the input and output images, respectively. The third input parameter is the threshold chosen. The meaning of `maxval` is controlled by the type of thresholding we want to perform. The following table shows the operation performed for each type:

Type	dst(x,y)
THRESH_BINARY	maxval if src(x,y) is greater than thresh and 0 if otherwise
THRESH_BINARY_INV	0 if src(x,y) is greater than thresh and maxval if otherwise
THRESH_TRUNC	thresh if src(x,y) is greater than thresh and src(x,y) if otherwise
THRESH_TOZERO	src(x,y) if src(x,y) is greater than thresh and 0 if otherwise
THRESH_TOZERO_INV	0 if src(x,y) is greater than thresh and src(x,y) if otherwise

While in previous OpenCV books (and the available reference manual) each type of thresholding is illustrated with the help of 1D signal plots, our experience shows that numbers and gray levels allow you to grasp the concept faster. The following table shows the effect of the different threshold types using a single-line image as an example input:

127	200	240	200	127	80	0	127

Sample image
top row: pixel values
bottom row: pixel intensities
thresh=127

0	255	255	255	0	0	0	0

Result of binary threshold
type=THRESH_BINARY
maxval=255

255	0	0	0	255	255	255	255

Result of inverted binary threshold
type=THRESH_BINARY_INV
maxval=255

127	127	127	127	127	80	0	127

Result of Truncate threshold
type=TRUNCATE
(maxval value is not used)

0	200	240	200	0	0	0	0

Result of Threshold to Zero
type=THRESH_TOZERO
(maxval value is not used)

127	0	0	0	127	80	0	127

Result of Threshold to Zero, inv.
type=THRESH_TOZERO_INV
(maxval value is not used)

The special value THRESH_OTSU may be combined with the previous values (with the OR operator). In such cases, the threshold value is automatically estimated by the function (using Otsu's algorithm). This function returns the estimated threshold value.

Otsu's method obtains a threshold that best separates the background from the foreground's pixels (in an interclass/intraclass variance ratio sense). See the full explanation and demos at http://www.labbookpages. co.uk/software/imgProc/otsuThreshold.html.

While the function described uses a single threshold for the whole image, adaptive thresholding estimates a different threshold for each pixel. This produces a better result when the input image is less homogeneous (with unevenly illuminated regions, for example). The function to perform adaptive thresholding is as follows:

```
adaptiveThreshold(InputArray src, OutputArray dst, double maxValue,
int adaptiveMethod, int thresholdType, int blockSize, double C)
```

This function is similar to the previous one. The parameter `thresholdType` must be either THRESH_BINARY or THRESH_BINARY_INV. This function computes a threshold for each pixel by computing a weighted average of pixels in a neighborhood minus a constant (C). When `thresholdType` is ADAPTIVE_THRESH_MEAN_C, the threshold computed is the mean of the neighborhood (that is, all the elements are weighted equally). When `thresholdType` is ADAPTIVE_THRESH_GAUSSIAN_C, the pixels in the neighborhood are weighted according to a Gaussian function.

The following `thresholding` example shows how to perform thresholding operations on an image:

```cpp
#include "opencv2/opencv.hpp"
#include <iostream>

using namespace std;
using namespace cv;

Mat src, dst, adaptDst;
int threshold_value, block_size, C;

void thresholding( int, void* )
{
   threshold( src, dst, threshold_value, 255, THRESH_BINARY );

   imshow( "Thresholding", dst );
}

void adaptThreshAndShow()
{
    adaptiveThreshold( src, adaptDst, 255, CV_ADAPTIVE_THRESH_MEAN_C,
      THRESH_BINARY, block_size, C);
    imshow( "Adaptive Thresholding", adaptDst );
}

void adaptiveThresholding1( int, void* )
{
  static int prev_block_size=block_size;
  if ((block_size%2)==0)     // make sure that block_size is odd
  {
      if (block_size>prev_block_size) block_size++;
```

```
        if (block_size<prev_block_size) block_size--;
    }
    if (block_size<=1) block_size=3;  // check block_size min value

    adaptThreshAndShow();
}

void adaptiveThresholding2( int, void* )
{
    adaptThreshAndShow();
}

int main(int argc, char *argv[])
{
    //Read original image and clone it to contain results
    src = imread("left12.jpg", CV_LOAD_IMAGE_GRAYSCALE );
    dst=src.clone();
    adaptDst=src.clone();

    //Create 3 windows
    namedWindow("Source", WINDOW_AUTOSIZE);
    namedWindow("Thresholding", WINDOW_AUTOSIZE);
    namedWindow("Adaptive Thresholding", WINDOW_AUTOSIZE);
    imshow("Source", src);

    //Create trackbars
    threshold_value=127;
    block_size=7;
    C=10;
    createTrackbar( "threshold", "Thresholding", &threshold_value,
        255, thresholding );
    createTrackbar( "block_size", "Adaptive Thresholding",
        &block_size, 25, adaptiveThresholding1 );
    createTrackbar( "C", "Adaptive Thresholding", &C, 255,
        adaptiveThresholding2 );

    //Perform operations a first time
    thresholding(threshold_value,0);
    adaptiveThresholding1(block_size, 0);
    adaptiveThresholding2(C, 0);

    // Position windows on screen
    moveWindow("Source", 0,0);
    moveWindow("Thresholding", src.cols,0);
    moveWindow("Adaptive Thresholding", 2*src.cols,0);

    cout << "Press any key to exit...\n";
    waitKey(); // Wait for key press
    return 0;
}
```

The example in the preceding code creates three windows with the source image, which is loaded in grayscale, and the result of thresholding and adaptive thresholding. Then, it creates three trackbars: one associated to the thresholding result window (to handle the threshold value) and two associated to the adaptive thresholding result window (to handle the block's size and the value of the constant C). Note that since two callback functions are necessary in this case, and we do not want to repeat code, the call to `adaptiveThreshold` is embedded in the function, `adaptThreshAndShow`.

Next, a call is made to the functions that perform the operations using default parameter values. Finally, the `moveWindow` function from `highgui` is used to reposition the windows on the screen (otherwise they will be displayed on top of each other, and only the third one will be visible). Also, note that the first six lines in the function `adaptiveThresholding1` are needed to keep an odd value in the parameter `block_size`. The following screenshot shows the output of the example:

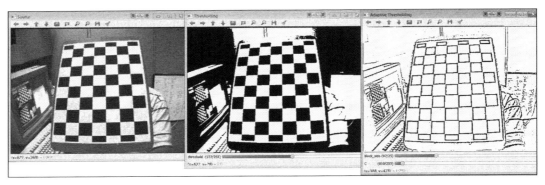

Output of the thresholding example

 The function `inRange(InputArray src, InputArray lowerb, InputArray upperb, OutputArray dst)` is also useful for thresholding as it checks whether the pixels lie between lower and upper thresholds. Both `lowerb` and `upperb` must be provided using Scalar, as in `inRange(src, Scalar(bl,gl,rl), Scalar(bh,gh,rh), tgt);`.

Contours and connected components

Contour extraction operations can be considered halfway between feature extraction and segmentation, since a binary image is produced in which image contours are separated from other homogeneous regions. Contours will typically correspond to object boundaries.

While a number of simple methods detect edges in images (for example, the Sobel and Laplace filters), the **Canny** method is a robust algorithm for doing this.

> This method uses two thresholds to decide whether a pixel is an edge. In what is called a hysteresis procedure, a lower and an upper threshold are used (see `http://docs.opencv.org/doc/tutorials/ imgproc/imgtrans/canny_detector/canny_detector.html`). Since OpenCV already includes a good example of the Canny edge detector (in `[opencv_source_code]/samples/cpp/edge.cpp`), we do not include one here (but see the following `floodFill` example). Instead, we will go on to describe other highly useful functions based on detected edges.

To detect straight lines, the Hough transform is a classical method. While the Hough transform method is available in OpenCV (the functions `HoughLines` and `HoughLinesP`, for example, `[opencv_source_code]/samples/cpp/houghlines. cpp`), the more recent **Line Segment Detector (LSD)** method is generally a more robust one. LSD works by finding alignments of high-gradient magnitude pixels, given its alignment tolerance feature. This method has been shown to be more robust and faster than the best previous Hough-based detector (Progressive Probabilistic Hough Transform).

The LSD method is not available in the 2.4.9 release of OpenCV; although, at the time of this writing, it is already available in the code source's repository in GitHub. The method will be available in Version 3.0. A short example (`[opencv_source_code]/ samples/cpp/lsd_lines.cpp`) in the library covers this functionality. However, we will provide an additional example that shows different features.

> To test the latest source code available in GitHub, go to `https://github.com/itseez/opencv` and download the library code as a ZIP file. Then, unzip it to a local folder and follow the same steps described in *Chapter 1, Getting Started*, to compile and install the library.

The LSD detector is a C++ class. The function `cv::Ptr<LineSegmentDetector>`
`cv::createLineSegmentDetector (int _refine=LSD_REFINE_STD, double`
`_scale=0.8, double_sigma_scale=0.6, double _quant=2.0, double _ang_`
`th=22.5, double _log_eps=0, double _density_th=0.7, int _n_bins=1024)`
creates an object of the class and returns a pointer to it. Note that several arguments
define the detector created. The meaning of those parameters requires you to know
the underlying algorithm, which is out of the scope of this book. Fortunately, the
default values will suffice for most purposes, so we refer the reader to the reference
manual (for Version 3.0 of the library) for special cases. Having said that, the first
parameter scale roughly controls the number of lines that are returned. The input
image is automatically rescaled by this factor. At lower resolutions, fewer lines
are detected.

 The `cv::Ptr<>` type is a template class for wrapping pointers. This
template is available in the 2.x API to facilitate automatic deallocation
using reference counting. The `cv:: Ptr<>` type is analogous to
`std::unique_ptr`.

Detection itself is accomplished with the method `LineSegmentDetector::`
`detect(const InputArray _image, OutputArray _lines, OutputArray`
`width=noArray(), OutputArray prec=noArray(), OutputArraynfa=noArray())`.
The first parameter is the input image, while the `_lines` array will be filled with a
(STL) vector of `Vec4i` objects that represent the (x, y) location of one end of the line
followed by the location of the other end. The optional parameters `width`, `prec`, and
`noArray` return additional information about the lines detected. The first one, `width`,
contains the estimated line widths. Lines can be drawn with the convenient (yet
simple) method called `LineSegmentDetector::drawSegments(InputOutputArray`
`_image, InputArray lines)`. Lines will be drawn on top of the input,
namely, `_image`.

The following `lineSegmentDetector` example shows the detector in action:

```
#include "opencv2/opencv.hpp"
#include <iostream>

using namespace std;
using namespace cv;

vector<Vec4i> lines;
vector<float> widths;
```

```
Mat input_image, output;

inline float line_length(const Point &a, const Point &b)
{
    return (sqrt((b.x-a.x)*(b.x-a.x) + (b.y-a.y)*(b.y-a.y)));
}


void MyDrawSegments(Mat &image, const vector<Vec4i>&lines, const
    vector<float>&widths,
const Scalar& color, const float length_threshold)
{
    Mat gray;
    if (image.channels() == 1)
    {
        gray = image;
    }
    else if (image.channels() == 3)
    {
        cvtColor(image, gray, COLOR_BGR2GRAY);
    }

    // Create a 3 channel image in order to draw colored lines
    std::vector<Mat> planes;
    planes.push_back(gray);
    planes.push_back(gray);
    planes.push_back(gray);

    merge(planes, image);

    // Draw segments if length exceeds threshold given
    for(int i = 0; i < lines.size(); ++i)
    {
        const Vec4i& v = lines[i];
        Point a(v[0], v[1]);
        Point b(v[2], v[3]);
        if (line_length(a,b) > length_threshold) line(image, a, b,
          color, widths[i]);
    }
}


void thresholding(int threshold, void*)
{
    input_image.copyTo(output);
```

```
        MyDrawSegments(output, lines, widths, Scalar(0, 255, 0),
          threshold);
        imshow("Detected lines", output);
    }

    int main(int argc, char** argv)
    {
        input_image = imread("building.jpg", IMREAD_GRAYSCALE);

        // Create an LSD detector object
      Ptr<LineSegmentDetector> ls = createLineSegmentDetector();

        // Detect the lines
    ls->detect(input_image, lines, widths);

        // Create window to show found lines
        output=input_image.clone();
        namedWindow("Detected lines", WINDOW_AUTOSIZE);

        // Create trackbar for line length threshold
        int threshold_value=50;
        createTrackbar( "Line length threshold", "Detected lines",
          &threshold_value, 1000, thresholding );
        thresholding(threshold_value, 0);

        waitKey();
        return 0;
    }
```

The preceding example creates a window with the source image, which is loaded in grayscale, and shows the drawSegments method. However, it allows you to impose a segment length threshold and specify the line colors (drawSegments will draw all the lines in red). Besides, lines will be drawn with a thickness given by the widths estimated by the detector. A trackbar is associated with the main window to control the length of the threshold. The following screenshot shows an output of the example:

Output of the lineSegmentDetector example

Circles can be detected using the function `HoughCircles(InputArray image, OutputArray circles, int method, double dp, double minDist, double param1=100, double param2=100, intminRadius=0, int maxRadius=0)`. The first parameter is a grayscale input image. Output parameter circles will be filled with a vector of `Vec3f` objects. Each object represents the `(center_x, center_y, radius)` components of a circle. The last two parameters represent the minimum and maximum search radii, so they have an effect on the number of circles detected. OpenCV already contains a straightforward example of this function, `[opencv_source_code]/samples/cpp/houghcircles.cpp`. The example detects circles with a radius between 1 and 30 and displays them on top of the input image.

Segmentation algorithms typically form connected components, that is, the regions of connected pixels in a binary image. In the following section, we show how to obtain connected components and their contours from a binary image. Contours can be retrieved using the now classical function, `findContours`. Examples of this function are available in the reference manual (also see the `[opencv_source_code]/samples/cpp/contours2.cpp` and `[opencv_source_code]/samples/cpp/segment_objects.cpp` examples). Also note that in the 3.0 release of OpenCV (and in the code already available in the GitHub repository), the class `ShapeDistanceExtractor` allows you to compare the contours with the Shape Context descriptor (an example of this is available at `[opencv_source_code]/samples/cpp/shape_example.cpp`) and the Hausdorff distance. This class is in a new module of the library called `shape`. Shape transformations are also available through the class `ShapeTransformer` (example, `[opencv_source_code]/samples/cpp/shape_transformation.cpp`).

The new functions `connectedComponents` and `connectedComponentsWithStats` retrieve connected components. These functions will be part of the 3.0 release, and they are already available in the GitHub repository. An example of this is included in OpenCV that shows how to use the first one, `[opencv_source_code]/samples/cpp/connected_components.cpp`.

 The connected component that labels the functionality was actually removed in previous OpenCV 2.4.x versions and has now been added again.

We provide another example (`connectedComponents`) that shows how to use the second function, `int connectedComponentsWithStats(InputArray image, OutputArray labels, OutputArray stats, OutputArray centroids, int connectivity=8, intltype=CV_32S)`, which provides useful statistics about each connected component. These statistics are accessed via `stats(label, column)` where the column can be the following table:

CC_STAT_LEFT	The leftmost (x) coordinate that is the inclusive start of the bounding box in the horizontal direction
CC_STAT_TOP	The topmost (y) coordinate that is the inclusive start of the bounding box in the vertical direction
CC_STAT_WIDTH	The horizontal size of the bounding box
CC_STAT_HEIGHT	The vertical size of the bounding box
CC_STAT_AREA	The total area (in pixels) of the connected component

The following is the code for the example:

```
#include <opencv2/core/utility.hpp>
#include "opencv2/imgproc.hpp"
#include "opencv2/highgui.hpp"
#include <iostream>

using namespace cv;
using namespace std;

Mat img;
int threshval = 227;

static void on_trackbar(int, void*)
{
    Mat bw = threshval < 128 ? (img < threshval) : (img >
      threshval);
    Mat labelImage(img.size(), CV_32S);

    Mat stats, centroids;
    int nLabels = connectedComponentsWithStats(bw, labelImage,
      stats, centroids);

    // Show connected components with random colors
    std::vector<Vec3b> colors(nLabels);
    colors[0] = Vec3b(0, 0, 0);//background
    for(int label = 1; label < nLabels; ++label){
        colors[label] = Vec3b( (rand()&200), (rand()&200),
          (rand()&200) );
    }
    Mat dst(img.size(), CV_8UC3);
    for(int r = 0; r < dst.rows; ++r){
        for(int c = 0; c < dst.cols; ++c){
            int label = labelImage.at<int>(r, c);
            Vec3b &pixel = dst.at<Vec3b>(r, c);
            pixel = colors[label];
        }
    }
    // Text labels with area of each cc (except background)
    for (int i=1; i< nLabels;i++)
    {
        float a=stats.at<int>(i,CC_STAT_AREA);
        Point org(centroids.at<double>(i,0),
          centroids.at<double>(i,1));
        String txtarea;
        std::ostringstream buff;
        buff << a;
        txtarea=buff.str();
        putText( dst, txtarea, org,FONT_HERSHEY_COMPLEX_SMALL, 1,
          Scalar(255,255,255), 1);
```

```
        }

        imshow( "Connected Components", dst );
    }

    int main( int argc, const char** argv )
    {
        img = imread("stuff.jpg", 0);
        namedWindow( "Connected Components", 1 );
        createTrackbar( "Threshold", "Connected Components",
            &threshval, 255, on_trackbar );
        on_trackbar(threshval, 0);

        waitKey(0);
        return 0;
    }
```

The preceding example creates a window with an associated trackbar. The trackbar controls the threshold to apply to the source image. Inside the on_trackbar function, a call is made to connectedComponentsWithStats using the result of the thresholding. This is followed by two sections of the code. The first section fills the pixels that correspond to each connected component with a random color. The pixels that belong to each component are in labelImage (a labelImage output is also given by the function connectedComponents). The second part displays a text with the area of each component. This text is positioned at the centroid of each component. The following screenshot shows the output of the example:

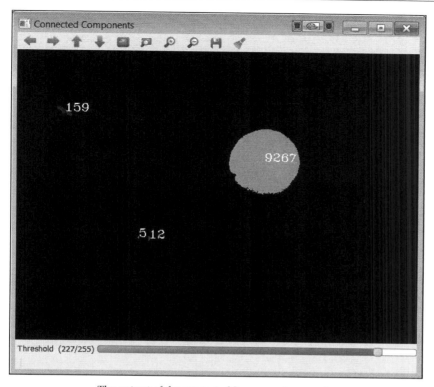

The output of the connectedComponents example

Flood fill

The flood fill operation fills the connected components with a given color. Starting from a seed point, the neighboring pixels are colored with a uniform color. The neighboring pixels can be within a specified range of the current pixel. The flood fill function is int floodFill(InputOutputArray image, Point seedPoint, Scalar newVal, Rect* rect=0, Scalar loDiff=Scalar(), Scalar upDiff=Scalar(),int flags=4). The parameters loDiff and upDiff represent the range to check for every neighboring pixel (note that 3-channel difference thresholds can be specified). The parameter newVal is the color to apply to the pixels that are in range. The lower part of the parameter flags contains the pixel's connectivity value to use (4 or 8). The upper part defines the mode of the operation.

Depending on this mode, the flood fill function will color a neighboring pixel in the input image if it is within the specified range (given by `loDiff` and `upDiff`) of either the current pixel or if the neighboring pixel is within the specified range of the original seed's value. The function can also be called with a mask image as the second parameter. If specified, the flood-filling operation will not go across non-zero pixels in the mask. Note that the mask should be a single-channel 8-bit image that is 2 pixels wider and 2 pixels taller than the input image.

The upper bit of `flags` can be 0 or a combination of the following:

- `FLOODFILL_FIXED_RANGE`: If set, the difference between the current pixel and seed pixel is considered. Otherwise, the difference between neighbor pixels is considered.

- `FLOODFILL_MASK_ONLY`: If set, the function does not change the image (`newVal` is ignored) but fills the mask.

In OpenCV's flood fill example (`[opencv_source_code]/samples/cpp/ffilldemo.cpp`), the mask is used only as an output parameter. In our `floodFill` example, shown as the following code, we will use it as an input parameter in order to constrain the filling. The idea is to use the output of an edge detector as a mask. This should stop the filling process at the edges:

```cpp
#include "opencv2/opencv.hpp"
#include <iostream>

using namespace std;
using namespace cv;

Mat image, image1, image_orig;
int loDiff = 20, upDiff = 30;
int loCanny=10, upCanny=150;

void onMouse( int event, int x, int y, int, void* )
{
    if( event != CV_EVENT_LBUTTONDOWN ) return;

    Point seed = Point(x,y);
    int flags = 4 + CV_FLOODFILL_FIXED_RANGE;
    int b = (unsigned)theRNG() & 255;
    int g = (unsigned)theRNG() & 255;
    int r = (unsigned)theRNG() & 255;
    Rect ccomp;

    Scalar newVal = Scalar(b, g, r);
```

```
    Mat dst = image;

    // flood fill
    floodFill(dst, seed, newVal, &ccomp, Scalar(loDiff, loDiff,
       loDiff), Scalar(upDiff, upDiff, upDiff), flags);
    imshow("image", dst);

    // Using Canny edges as mask
    Mat mask;
    Canny(image_orig, mask, loCanny, upCanny);
    imshow("Canny edges", mask);
    copyMakeBorder(mask, mask, 1, 1, 1, 1, cv::BORDER_REPLICATE);
    Mat dst1 = image1;
    floodFill(dst1, mask, seed, newVal, &ccomp, Scalar(loDiff,
       loDiff, loDiff), Scalar(upDiff, upDiff, upDiff), flags);
    imshow("FF with Canny", dst1);

    moveWindow("Canny edges", image.cols,0);
    moveWindow("FF with Canny", 2*image.cols,0);
}

int main(int argc, char *argv[])
{
    // Read original image and clone it to contain results
    image = imread("lena.jpg", CV_LOAD_IMAGE_COLOR );
    image_orig=image.clone();
    image1=image.clone();

    namedWindow( "image", WINDOW_AUTOSIZE );

    imshow("image", image);
    createTrackbar( "lo_diff", "image", &loDiff, 255, 0 );
    createTrackbar( "up_diff", "image", &upDiff, 255, 0 );
    createTrackbar( "lo_Canny", "image", &loCanny, 255, 0 );
    createTrackbar( "up_Canny", "image", &upCanny, 255, 0 );
    setMouseCallback( "image", onMouse, 0 );

    moveWindow("image", 0,0);

    cout << "Press any key to exit...\n";
    waitKey(); // Wait for key press
    return 0;
}
```

The preceding example reads and displays a color image and then creates four trackbars. The first two trackbars control `loDiff` and `upDiff` values for the `floodFill` function. The other two trackbars control the lower and upper threshold parameters for the Canny edge detector. In this example, the user can click anywhere on the input image. The click position will be used as a seed point to perform a flood fill operation. Actually, upon each click, two calls are made to the `floodFill` function. The first one simply fills a region using a random color. The second one uses a mask created from the output of the Canny edge detector. Note that the `copyMakeBorder` function is necessary to form a 1-pixel wide border around the mask. The following screenshot shows the output of this example:

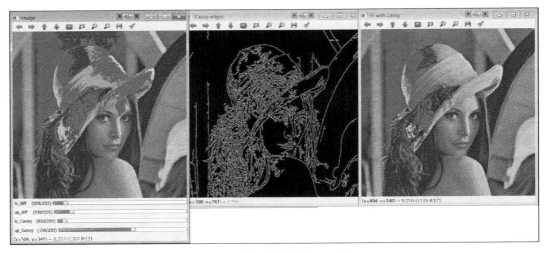

Output of the floodFill example

Note that the output that uses Canny edges (right) has filled in less pixels than the standard operation (left).

Watershed segmentation

Watershed is a segmentation method that is known for its efficiency. The method essentially starts from user-specified starting (seed) points from which regions grow. Assuming that good starting seeds can be provided, the resulting segmentations are useful for many purposes.

> For more details and examples about the watershed transform for image segmentation, see `http://cmm.ensmp.fr/~beucher/wtshed.html`.

The function `watershed(InputArray image, InputOutputArray markers)` accepts a 3-channel input image and an image called `markers` with the seeds. The latter has to be a 32-bit single-channel image. Seeds may be specified in `markers` as connected components with positive values (0 cannot be used as a value for seeds). As an output argument, each pixel in `markers` will be set to a value of the seed components or `-1` at boundaries between the regions. OpenCV includes a watershed example (`[opencv_source_code]/samples/cpp/watershed.cpp`) in which the user has to draw the seed's regions.

Obviously, the selection of the seed regions is important. Ideally, seeds will be selected automatically without user intervention. A typical use of watershed is to first threshold the image to separate the object from the background, apply the distance transform, and then use the local maxima of the distance transform image as seed points for segmentation. However, the first thresholding step is critical, as parts of the object may be considered as the background. In this case, the object seed region will be too small and segmentation will be poor. On the other hand, to perform a watershed segmentation, we need seeds for the background too. While we can use points over the corners of the image as seeds, this will not be sufficient. In this case, the background seed region is too small. If we use those seeds, the object region given by the segmentation will be generally much larger than the real object. In our following watershed example, a different approach is followed that produces better results:

```cpp
#include <opencv2/core/utility.hpp>
#include "opencv2/imgproc.hpp"
#include "opencv2/highgui.hpp"
#include "opencv2/core.hpp"
#include <iostream>

using namespace std;
using namespace cv;


void Watershed(const Mat &src)
{
    Mat dst=src.clone();

    // Flood fill outer part of the image
    Point seed(0,0); // top-left corner
    int loDiff=20;
    int upDiff=20;
    int flags=4 + FLOODFILL_FIXED_RANGE + FLOODFILL_MASK_ONLY +
(255<<8);
    Mat mask(src.size(), CV_8UC1);
    mask.setTo(0);
    copyMakeBorder(mask, mask, 1, 1, 1, 1, cv::BORDER_REPLICATE);
    Scalar newVal;
```

```
        Rect ccomp;
        floodFill(dst, mask, seed, newVal, &ccomp,
               Scalar(loDiff, loDiff, loDiff), Scalar(upDiff, upDiff,
    upDiff), flags);

        // Flood fill inner part of the image
        seed.x=(float)src.cols/2;    // image center x
        seed.y=(float)src.rows/2;    // image center y
        Mat mask1=mask.clone();
        mask1.setTo(0);
        floodFill(dst, mask1, seed, newVal, &ccomp,
               Scalar(loDiff, loDiff, loDiff), Scalar(upDiff, upDiff,
    upDiff), flags);

        // Form image with the two seed regions
        Mat Mask = mask.clone();
        mask=mask/2;
        Mask = mask | mask1;
        imshow("Seed regions", Mask);
        moveWindow("Seed regions", src.cols, 0);

        // Perform watershed
        Mat labelImage(src.size(), CV_32SC1);
        labelImage=Mask(Rect(1,1, src.cols, src.rows));
        labelImage.convertTo(labelImage, CV_32SC1);
        watershed(src, labelImage);
        labelImage.convertTo(labelImage, CV_8U);
        imshow("Watershed", labelImage);
        moveWindow("Watershed", 2*src.cols, 0);
    }


    int main(int argc, char *argv[])
    {
        // Read original image and clone it to contain results
        Mat src = imread("hand_sample2.jpg", IMREAD_COLOR );

        // Create 3 windows
        namedWindow("Source", WINDOW_AUTOSIZE);
        imshow("Source", src);

        Watershed(src);

        // Position windows on screen
        moveWindow("Source", 0,0);

        cout << "Press any key to exit...\n";
        waitKey(); // Wait for key press
        return 0;
    }
```

The `Watershed` function in the preceding code performs three steps. First, a background seed region is obtained by performing a flood fill. The flood fill seed is the upper left corner of the image, that is, pixel (0, 0). Next, another flood fill is performed to obtain an object's (hand in the sample image) seed region. The seed for this flood fill is taken as the center of the image. Then, a seed region image is formed by performing an OR operation between the previous two flood fill results. The resulting image is used as the seed image for the watershed operation. See the output of the example in the following screenshot where the seed image is shown at the center of the figure:

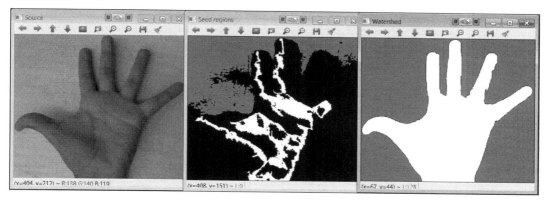

The output of the watershed example

GrabCut

GrabCut is an excellent iterative background/foreground segmentation algorithm that is available since Version 2.1 of OpenCV. GrabCut is especially useful to separate objects from the background with minimal additional information (a bounding rectangle is sufficient in most cases). However, it is computationally intensive, and so it is only appropriate to segment still images.

GrabCut is the underlying algorithm for the Background Removal tool in Microsoft Office 2010. This algorithm was first proposed by researchers at Microsoft Research Cambridge. Starting with a user-provided bounding box of the object to segment, the algorithm estimates the color distributions of both the target object and the background. This estimate is further refined by minimizing an energy function in which connected regions that have the same label receive more weight.

The main function is grabCut(InputArray img, InputOutputArray mask, Rect rect, InputOutputArray bgdModel, InputOutputArray fgdModel, int iterCount, int mode=GC_EVAL). The parameters bgdModel and fgdModel are only used internally by the function (though they have to be declared). The iterCount variable is the number of iterations to be performed. In our experience, few iterations of the algorithm are required to produce good segmentations. The algorithm is aided by a bounding rectangle, a mask image, or both. The option chosen is indicated in the mode parameter, which can be GC_INIT_WITH_RECT, GC_INIT_WITH_MASK, or an OR combination of the two. In the former case, rect defines the rectangle. Pixels outside the rectangle are considered as the obvious background. In the latter case, the mask is an 8-bit image in which pixels may have the following values:

- GC_BGD: This defines an obvious background pixel
- GC_FGD: This defines an obvious foreground (object) pixel
- GC_PR_BGD: This defines a possible background pixel
- GC_PR_FGD: This defines a possible foreground pixel

The image mask is also the output image with the resulting segmentation, which is derived using those same previous values. OpenCV includes an example of GrabCut ([opencv_source_code]/samples/cpp/grabcut.cpp) in which the user can draw a bounding rectangle as well as foreground and background pixels.

The following grabcut example uses the algorithm with an initial bounding rectangle and then copies the resulting foreground onto another position in the same image:

```cpp
#include "opencv2/opencv.hpp"
#include <iostream>

using namespace std;
using namespace cv;

int main(int argc, char *argv[])
{
    // Read original image and clone it
    Mat src = imread("stuff.jpg" );
    Mat tgt = src.clone();

    // Create source window
    namedWindow("Source", WINDOW_AUTOSIZE);
```

```
imshow("Source", src);
moveWindow("Source", 0,0);

// GrabCut segmentation
Rect rectangle(180,279,60,60);    // coin position
Mat result;                       // segmentation result
Mat bgModel,fgModel;              // used internally
grabCut(src, result, rectangle, bgModel,fgModel, 1, GC_INIT_WITH_
RECT);

result=(result & GC_FGD);    // leave only obvious foreground

// Translation operation
Mat aff=Mat::eye(2,3,CV_32FC1);
aff.at<float>(0,2)=50;
warpAffine(tgt, src, aff, result.size());
warpAffine(result, result, aff, result.size());
src.copyTo(tgt, result);

// Show target window
imshow("Target", tgt);
moveWindow("Target", src.cols, 0);

cout << "Press any key to exit...\n";
waitKey(); // Wait for key press
return 0;
}
```

The preceding example simply uses a fixed rectangle around the coin in the source image (see the fifth screenshot in this chapter) and performs the segmentation. The `result` image will contain values between 0 (GC_BGD) and 3 (GC_PR_FGD). The ensuing AND operation is needed to convert values other than GC_FGD to zero and thus get a binary foreground mask. Then, both the source image and the mask are translated by 50 pixels in the horizontal. An affine warping operation is used with an identity matrix in which only the x translation component is changed.

Finally, the translated image is copied onto the target image, using the (also translated) mask. Both source and target images are shown in the following screenshot. Increasing the number of iterations did not have any significant effect in this particular example:

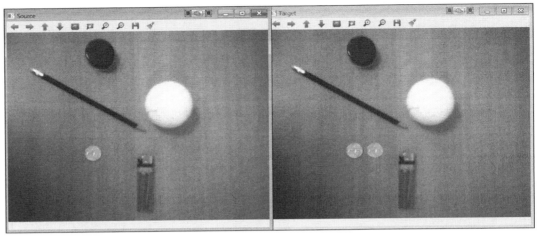

Source and target images in the GrabCut example

Summary

This chapter has covered one of the most important subjects in computer vision. Segmentation is often one of the first steps, and also, it is typically one of the trickiest. In this chapter, we have provided the reader with insight and samples to use the most useful segmentation methods in OpenCV, such as thresholding, contours and connected components, flood filling of regions, the watershed segmentation method, and the GrabCut method.

What else?

The meanshift segmentation (the function `pyrMeanShiftFiltering`) has been omitted. OpenCV includes an example showing how to use this function (`[opencv_source_code]/samples/cpp/meanshift_segmentation.cpp`).This method is, however, relatively slow and tends to produce oversegmented results.

Background/foreground segmentations can also be achieved using video, which will be covered in *Chapter 7, What Is He Doing? Motion*.

5
Focusing on the Interesting 2D Features

In most images, the most useful information is around certain zones that typically correspond to salient points and regions. In most applications, local processing around these salient points is sufficient as long as these points are stable and distinctive. In this chapter, we will cover a basic introduction to the 2D salient points and features offered by OpenCV. It is important to note the difference between detectors and descriptors. **Detectors** only extract interest points (local features) on an image, while descriptors obtain relevant information about the neighborhood of these points. **Descriptors**, as their name suggests, describe the image by proper features. They describe an interest point in a way that is invariant to change in lighting and to small perspective deformations. This can be used to match them with other descriptors (typically extracted from other images). For this purpose, matchers are used. This, in turn, can be used to detect objects and infer the camera transformation between two images. First, we show the internal structure of the interest points and provide an explanation of the 2D features and descriptor extraction. Finally, the chapter deals with matching, that is, putting 2D features of different images into correspondence.

Interest points

Local features, also called interest points, are characterized by sudden changes of intensity in the region. These local features are usually classified in edges, corners, and blobs. OpenCV encapsulates interesting point information in the `KeyPoint` class, which contains the following data:

- The coordinates of the interest point (the `Point2f` type)
- Diameter of the meaningful keypoint neighborhood
- Orientation of the keypoint
- Strength of the keypoint, which depends on the keypoint detector that is selected
- Pyramid layer (octave) from which the keypoint has been extracted; octaves are used in some descriptors such as `SIFT`, `SURF`, `FREAK`, or `BRISK`
- Object ID used to perform clustering

Feature detectors

OpenCV handles several local feature detector implementations through the `FeatureDetector` abstract class and its `Ptr<FeatureDetector>` `FeatureDetector::create(const string& detectorType)` method or through the algorithm class directly. In the first case, the type of detector is specified (see the following diagram where the detectors used in this chapter are indicated in red color). Detectors and the types of local features that they detect are as follows:

- FAST (`FastFeatureDetector`): This feature detects corners and blobs
- STAR (`StarFeatureDetector`): This feature detects edges, corners, and blobs
- SIFT (`SiftFeatureDetector`): This feature detects corners and blobs (part of the `nonfree` module)
- SURF (`SurfFeatureDetector`): This feature detects corners and blobs (part of the `nonfree` module)
- ORB (`OrbFeatureDetector`): This feature detects corners and blobs
- BRISK (`BRISK`): This feature detects corners and blobs
- MSER (`MserFeatureDetector`): This feature detects blobs
- GFTT (`GoodFeaturesToTrackDetector`): This feature detects edges and corners

- HARRIS (GoodFeaturesToTrackDetector): This feature detects edges and corners (with the Harris detector enabled)

- Dense (DenseFeatureDetector): This feature detects the features that are distributed densely and regularly on the image

- SimpleBlob (SimpleBlobDetector): This feature detects blobs

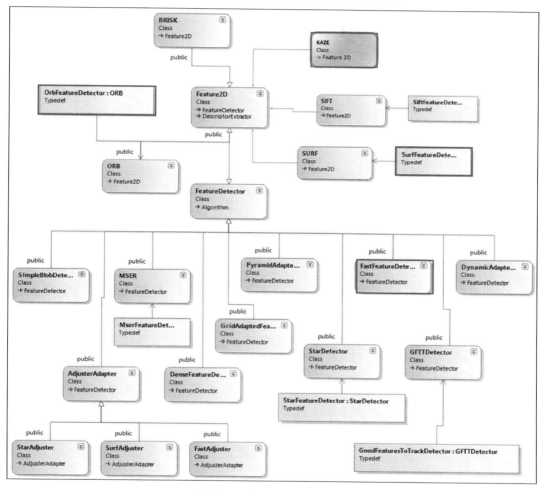

2D feature detectors in OpenCV

We should note that some of these detectors, such as SIFT, SURF, ORB, and BRISK, are also descriptors.

Keypoint detection is performed by the `void FeatureDetector::detect(const Mat& image, vector<KeyPoint>& keypoints, const Mat& mask)` function, which is another method of the `FeatureDetector` class. The first parameter is the input image where the keypoints will be detected. The second parameter corresponds to the vector where the keypoints will be stored. The last parameter is optional and represents an input mask image in which we can specify where to look for keypoints.

Matthieu Labbé has implemented a Qt-based open source application where you can test OpenCV's corner detectors, feature extractors, and matching algorithms in a nice GUI. It is available at `https://code.google.com/p/find-object/`.

The first interest points were historically corners. In 1977, Moravec defined corners as interest points where there is a large intensity variation in several directions (45 degrees). These interest points were used by Moravec to find matching regions in consecutive image frames. Later, in 1988, Harris improved Moravec's algorithm using the Taylor expansion to approximate the shifted intensity variation. Afterwards, other detectors appeared, such as the detector based on **difference of Gaussians (DoG)** and **determinant of the Hessian (DoH)** (for example, SIFT or SURF, respectively) or the detector based on Moravec's algorithm, but considering continuous intensity values in a pixel neighborhood such as FAST or BRISK (scale-space FAST).

Lu, in her personal blog, *LittleCheeseCake*, explains some of the most popular detectors and descriptors in detail. The blog is available at `http://littlecheesecake.me/blog/13804625/feature-detectors-and-descriptors`.

The FAST detector

The corner detector is based on the **Features from Accelerated Segment Test (FAST)** algorithm. It was designed to be very efficient, targeting real-time applications. The method is based on considering a circle of 16 pixels (neighborhood) around a candidate corner p. The FAST detector will consider p as a corner if there is a set of contiguous pixels in the neighborhood that all are brighter than p+T or darker than p-T, T being a threshold value. This threshold must be properly selected.

OpenCV implements the FAST detector in the FastFeatureDetector() class, which is a wrapper class for the FAST() method. To use this class, we must include the features2d.hpp header file in our code.

Next, we show a code example where the corners are detected using the FAST method with different threshold values. The FASTDetector code example is shown as follows:

```cpp
#include "opencv2/core/core.hpp"
#include "opencv2/highgui/highgui.hpp"
#include "opencv2/imgproc/imgproc.hpp"
#include "opencv2/features2d/features2d.hpp"
#include <iostream>

using namespace std;
using namespace cv;

int main(int argc, char *argv[])
{
    //Load original image and convert to gray scale
    Mat in_img = imread("book.png");
    cvtColor( in_img, in_img, COLOR_BGR2GRAY );

    //Create a keypoint vectors
    vector<KeyPoint> keypoints1,keypoints2;
    //FAST detector with threshold value of 80 and 100
    FastFeatureDetector detector1(80);
    FastFeatureDetector detector2(100);

    //Compute keypoints in in_img with detector1 and detector2
    detector1.detect(in_img, keypoints1);
    detector2.detect(in_img, keypoints2);

    Mat out_img1, out_img2;
    //Draw keypoints1 and keypoints2
    drawKeypoints(in_img,keypoints1,out_img1,Scalar::all(-1),0);
    drawKeypoints(in_img,keypoints2,out_img2,Scalar::all(-1),0);

    //Show keypoints detected by detector1 and detector2
    imshow( "out_img1", out_img1 );
    imshow( "out_img2", out_img2 );
    waitKey(0);
    return 0;
}
```

The explanation of the code is given as follows. In this and the following examples, we usually perform the following three steps:

1. Create the 2D feature detector.
2. Detect keypoints in the image.
3. Draw the keypoints obtained.

In our sample, `FastFeatureDetector(int threshold=1, bool nonmaxSuppression= true, type=FastFeatureDetector::TYPE_9_16)` is the function where the detector parameters, such as threshold value, non-maximum suppression, and neighborhoods, are defined.

The following three types of neighborhoods can be selected:

*   `FastFeatureDetector::TYPE_9_16`
*   `FastFeatureDetector::TYPE_7_12`
*   `FastFeatureDetector::TYPE_5_8`

These neighborhoods define the number of neighbors (16, 12, or 8) and the total number of contiguous pixels (9, 7, or 5) needed to consider the corner (keypoint) valid. An example of `TYPE_9_16` is shown in the next screenshot.

In our code, the threshold values `80` and `100` have been selected, while the rest of the parameters have their default values, `nonmaxSuppression=true` and `type=FastFeatureDetector::TYPE_9_16`, as shown:

```
FastFeatureDetector detector1(80);
FastFeatureDetector detector2(100);
```

Keypoints are detected and saved using the `void detect(const Mat& image, vector<KeyPoint>& keypoints, const Mat& mask=Mat())` function. In our case, we create the following two FAST feature detectors:

*   `detector1` saves its keypoints in the `keypoints1` vector
*   `detector2` saves its keypoints in the `keypoints2`

The `void drawKeypoints(const Mat& image, const vector<KeyPoint>& keypoints, Mat& outImage, const Scalar& color=Scalar::all(-1), int flags=DrawMatchesFlags::DEFAULT)` function draws the keypoints in the image. The `color` parameter allows us to define a color of keypoints, and with the `Scalar:: all(-1)` option, each keypoint will be drawn with a different color.

The keypoints are drawn using the two threshold values on the image. We will notice a small difference in the number of keypoints detected. This is due to the threshold value in each case. The following screenshot shows a corner detected in the sample with a threshold value of 80, which is not detected with a threshold value of 100:

Keypoint detected with a threshold value of 80 (in the left-hand side). The same corner is not detected with a threshold value of 100 (in the right-hand side).

The difference is due to the fact that the FAST feature detectors are created with the default type, that is, TYPE_9_16. In the example, the p pixel takes a value of 228, so at least nine contiguous pixels must be brighter than p+T or darker than p-T. The following screenshot shows the neighborhood pixel values in this specific keypoint. The condition of nine contiguous pixels is met if we use a threshold value of 80. However, the condition is not met with a threshold value of 100:

50	70	131	121	131	130	134
49	71	175	191	132	135	134
49	70	177	223	219	160	139
50	72	170	288	225	221	214
53	70	131	180	224	223	225
55	74	118	149	153	209	228
57	82	108	154	151	146	174

Keypoint pixel values and contiguous pixels all darker than p-T (228-80=148) with a threshold value of 80

The SURF detector

The **Speeded Up Robust Features** (SURF) detector is based on a Hessian matrix to find the interest points. For this purpose, SURF divides the image in different scales (levels and octaves) using second-order Gaussian kernels and approximates these kernels with a simple box filter. This filter box is mostly interpolated in scale and space in order to provide the detector with the scale-invariance properties. SURF is a faster approximation of the classic **Scale Invariant Feature Transform** (SIFT) detector. Both the SURF and SIFT detectors are patented, so OpenCV includes them separately in their `nonfree/nonfree.hpp` header file.

The following `SURFDetector` code shows an example where the keypoints are detected using the SURF detector with a different number of Gaussian pyramid octaves:

```
//… (omitted for simplicity)
#include "opencv2/nonfree/nonfree.hpp"

int main(int argc, char *argv[])
{
    //Load image and convert to gray scale (omitted for
    //simplicity)

    //Create a keypoint vectors
    vector<KeyPoint> keypoints1,keypoints2;

    //SURF detector1 and detector2 with 2 and 5 Gaussian pyramid
    //octaves respectively
    SurfFeatureDetector detector1(3500, 2, 2, false, false);
    SurfFeatureDetector detector2(3500, 5, 2, false, false);

    //Compute keypoints in in_img with detector1 and detector2
    detector1.detect(in_img, keypoints1);
    detector2.detect(in_img, keypoints2);
    Mat out_img1, out_img2;

    //Draw keypoints1 and keypoints2
    drawKeypoints(in_img,keypoints1,out_img1,Scalar::all(-1),
        DrawMatchesFlags::DRAW_RICH_KEYPOINTS);
    drawKeypoints(in_img,keypoints2,out_img2,Scalar::all(-1),
        DrawMatchesFlags::DRAW_RICH_KEYPOINTS);

    //Show the 2 final images (omitted for simplicity)
    return 0;
}
```

In the preceding example (and subsequent ones), some portions of code are not repeated for simplicity because they are the same as in previous examples.

The explanation of the code is given as follows. SURFFeatureDetector(double hessianThreshold, int nOctaves, int nOctaveLayers, bool extended, bool upright) is the main function used to create a SURF detector where we can define the parameter values of the detector, such as the Hessian threshold, the number of Gaussian pyramid octaves, number of images within each octave of a Gaussian pyramid, number of elements in the descriptor, and the orientation of each feature.

A high threshold value extracts less keypoints but with more accuracy. A low threshold value extracts more keypoints but with less accuracy. In this case, we have used a large Hessian threshold (3500) to show a reduced number of keypoints in the image. Also, the number of octaves changes for each image (2 and 5, respectively). A larger number of octaves also select keypoints with a larger size. The following screenshot shows the result:

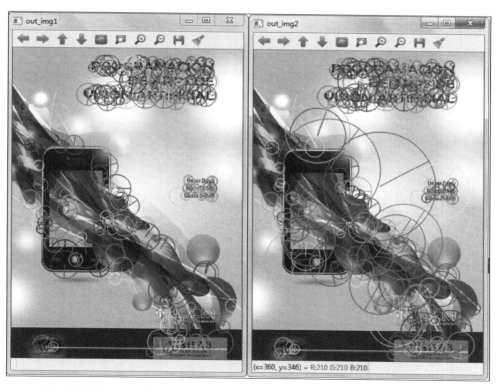

The SURF detector with two Gaussian pyramid octaves (in the left-hand side) and the SURF detector with five Gaussian pyramid octaves (in the right-hand side)

Again, we use the `drawKeypoints` function to draw the keypoints detected, but in this case, as the SURF detector has orientation properties, the `DrawMatchesFlags` parameter is defined as `DRAW_RICH_KEYPOINTS`. Then, the `drawKeypoints` function draws each keypoint with its size and orientation.

The ORB detector

Binary Robust Independent Elementary Features (BRIEF) is a descriptor based on binary strings; it does not find interest points. The **Oriented FAST and Rotated BRIEF (ORB)** detector is a union of the FAST detector and BRIEF descriptor and is considered an alternative to the patented SIFT and SURF detectors. The ORB detector uses the FAST detector with pyramids to detect interest points and then uses the HARRIS algorithm to rank the features and retain the best ones. OpenCV also allows us to use the FAST algorithm to rank the features, but normally, this produces less stable keypoints. The following `ORBDetector` code shows a simple and clear example of this difference:

```
int main(int argc, char *argv[])
{
    //Load image and convert to gray scale (omitted for
    //simplicity)

    //Create a keypoint vectors
    vector<KeyPoint> keypoints1,keypoints2;

    //ORB detector with FAST (detector1) and HARRIS (detector2)
    //score to rank the features
    OrbFeatureDetector detector1(300, 1.1f, 2, 31,0, 2,
        ORB::FAST_SCORE, 31);
    OrbFeatureDetector detector2(300, 1.1f, 2, 31,0, 2,
        ORB::HARRIS_SCORE, 31);

    //Compute keypoints in in_img with detector1 and detector2
    detector1.detect(in_img, keypoints1);
    detector2.detect(in_img, keypoints2);

    Mat out_img1, out_img2;
    //Draw keypoints1 and keypoints2
    drawKeypoints(in_img,keypoints1,out_img1,Scalar::all(-1),
        DrawMatchesFlags::DEFAULT);
    drawKeypoints(in_img,keypoints2,out_img2,Scalar::all(-1),
        DrawMatchesFlags::DEFAULT);

    //Show the 2 final images (omitted for simplicity)
    return 0;
}
```

The ORB detector with the FAST algorithm to select the 300 best features (in the left-hand side) and the HARRIS detector to select the 300 best features (in the right-hand side)

The explanation of the code is given as follows. The `OrbFeatureDetector(int nfeatures=500, float scaleFactor=1.2f, int nlevels=8, int edgeThreshold=31, int firstLevel=0, int WTA_K=2, int scoreType=ORB::HARRIS_SCORE, int patchSize=31)` function is the class constructor where we can specify the maximum number of features to retain the scale, number of levels, and type of detector (`HARRIS_SCORE` or `FAST_SCORE`) used to rank the features.

The following proposed code example shows the difference between the HARRIS and FAST algorithms to rank features; the result is shown in the preceding screenshot:

```
OrbFeatureDetector detector1(300, 1.1f, 2, 31,0, 2,
   ORB::FAST_SCORE, 31);
OrbFeatureDetector detector2(300, 1.1f, 2, 31,0, 2,
   ORB::HARRIS_SCORE, 31);
```

The HARRIS corner detector is used more than FAST to rank features, because it rejects edges and provides a reasonable score. The rest of the functions are the same as in the previous detector examples, keypoint detection and drawing.

The KAZE and AKAZE detectors

The KAZE and AKAZE detectors will be included in the upcoming OpenCV 3.0.

 OpenCV 3.0 is not yet available. Again, if you want to test this code and use the KAZE and AKAZE features, you can work with the latest version already available in the OpenCV git repository at http://code.opencv.org/projects/opencv/repository.

The KAZE detector is a method that can detect 2D features in a nonlinear scale space. This method allows us to keep important image details and remove noise. **Additive Operator Splitting (AOS)** schemes are used for nonlinear scale space. AOS schemes are efficient, stable, and parallelizable. The algorithm computes the response of a Hessian matrix at multiple scale levels to detect keypoints. On the other hand, the **Accelerated-KAZE (AKAZE)** feature detector uses fast explicit diffusion to build a nonlinear scale space.

Next, in the KAZEDetector code, we see an example of the new KAZE and AKAZE feature detectors:

```
int main(int argc, char *argv[])
{
    //Load image and convert to gray scale (omitted for
    //simplicity)

    //Create a keypoint vectors
    vector<KeyPoint> keypoints1,keypoints2;

    //Create KAZE and AKAZE detectors
    KAZE detector1(true,true);
    AKAZE detector2(cv::AKAZE::DESCRIPTOR_KAZE_UPRIGHT,0,3);

    //Compute keypoints in in_img with detector1 and detector2
    detector1.detect(in_img, keypoints1);
    detector2.detect(in_img, keypoints2,cv::Mat());

    Mat out_img1, out_img2;
    //Draw keypoints1 and keypoints2
    drawKeypoints(in_img,keypoints1,out_img1,Scalar::all(-1),
        DrawMatchesFlags::DRAW_RICH_KEYPOINTS);
```

```
drawKeypoints(in_img,keypoints2,out_img2,Scalar::all(-1),
    DrawMatchesFlags::DRAW_RICH_KEYPOINTS);

//Show the 2 final images (omitted for simplicity)
return 0;
}
```

The `KAZE::KAZE(bool extended, bool upright)` function is the KAZE class constructor in which two parameters can be selected: `extended` and `upright`. The `extended` parameter adds the option to select between 64 or 128 descriptors, while the `upright` parameter allows us to select rotation or no invariant. In this case, we use both parameters with a `true` value.

On the other hand, the `AKAZE::AKAZE(DESCRIPTOR_TYPE descriptor_type, int descriptor_size=0, int descriptor_channels=3)` function is the AKAZE class constructor. This function gets the descriptor type, descriptor size, and the channels as input arguments. For the descriptor type, the following enumeration is applied:

```
enum DESCRIPTOR_TYPE {DESCRIPTOR_KAZE_UPRIGHT = 2, DESCRIPTOR_KAZE
    = 3, DESCRIPTOR_MLDB_UPRIGHT = 4, DESCRIPTOR_MLDB = 5 };
```

The following screenshot shows the results obtained with this example:

The KAZE detector (in the left-hand side) and the AKAZE detector (in the right-hand side)

Eugene Khvedchenya's *Computer Vision Talks* blog contains useful reports that compare different keypoints in terms of robustness and efficiency. See the posts at `http://computer-vision-talks.com/articles/2012-08-18-a-battle-of-three-descriptors-surf-freak-and-brisk/` and `http://computer-vision-talks.com/articles/2011-07-13-comparison-of-the-opencv-feature-detection-algorithms/`.

Feature descriptor extractors

Descriptors describe local image regions and are invariant to image transformations such as rotation, scale or translation. They provide a measure and distance function for a small patch around an interest point. Therefore, whenever the similarity between two image patches needs to be estimated, we compute their descriptors and measure their distance. In OpenCV, the basic Mat type is used to represent a collection of descriptors, where each row is a keypoint descriptor.

There are the following two possibilities to use a feature descriptor extractor:

- The `DescriptorExtractor` common interface
- The algorithm class directly

(See the following diagram where the descriptors used in this chapter are indicated in red color.)

The common interface allows us to switch easily between different algorithms. This can be very useful when choosing an algorithm to solve a problem, as the results of each algorithm can be compared with no effort. On the other hand, depending on the algorithm, there are several parameters that can be tweaked only using its class.

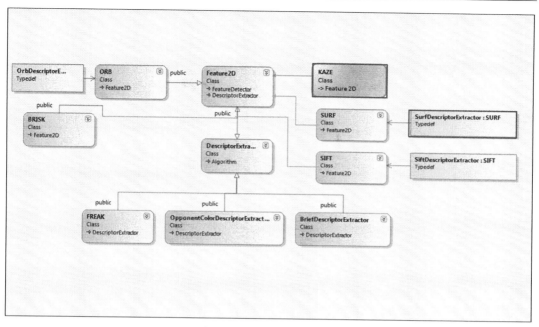

2D feature descriptors in OpenCV

The `Ptr<DescriptorExtractor> DescriptorExtractor::create(const String& descriptorExtractorType)` function creates a new descriptor extractor of the selected type. Descriptors can be grouped in two families: float and binary. Float descriptors store float values in a vector; this can lead to a high memory usage. On the other hand, binary descriptors store binary strings, thus enabling faster processing times and a reduced memory footprint. The current implementation supports the following types:

- SIFT: This implementation supports the float descriptor
- SURF: This implementation supports the float descriptor
- BRIEF: This implementation supports the binary descriptor
- BRISK: This implementation supports the binary descriptor
- ORB: This implementation supports the binary descriptor
- FREAK: This implementation supports the binary descriptor
- KAZE: This implementation supports the binary descriptor (new in OpenCV 3.0)
- AKAZE: This implementation supports the binary descriptor (new in OpenCV 3.0)

The other important function of `DescriptorExtractor` is `void DescriptorE xtractor::compute(InputArray image, vector<KeyPoint>& keypoints, OutputArray descriptors)`, which computes the descriptors for a set of keypoints detected in an image on the previous step. There is a variant of the function that accepts an image set.

 Note that it is possible to mix feature detectors and descriptor extractors from different algorithms. However, it is recommended that you use both methods from the same algorithm, as they should fit better together.

Descriptor matchers

`DescriptorMatcher` is an abstract base class to match keypoint descriptors that, as happens with `DescriptorExtractor`, make programs more flexible than using matchers directly. With the `Ptr<DescriptorMatcher> DescriptorMatcher::create(const string& descriptorMatcherType)` function, we can create a descriptor matcher of the desired type. The following are the supported types:

- **BruteForce-L1**: This is used for float descriptors. It uses L1 distance and is efficient and fast.
- **BruteForce**: This is used for float descriptors. It uses L2 distance and can be better than L1, but it needs more CPU usage.
- **BruteForce-SL2**: This is used for float descriptors and avoids square root computation from L2, which requires high CPU usage.
- **BruteForce-Hamming**: This is used for binary descriptors and calculates the Hamming distance between the compared descriptors.
- **BruteForce-Hamming(2)**: This is used for binary descriptors (2 bits version).
- **FlannBased**: This is used for float descriptors and is faster than brute force by pre-computing acceleration structures (as in DB engines) at the cost of using more memory.

The `void DescriptorMatcher::match(InputArray queryDescriptors, InputArray trainDescriptors, vector<DMatch>& matches, InputArray mask=noArray())` and `void DescriptorMatcher::knnMat ch(InputArray queryDescriptors, InputArray trainDescriptors, vector<vector<DMatch>>& matches, int k, InputArray mask=noArray(), bool compactResult=false)` functions give the best k matches for each descriptor, k being 1 for the first function.

The `void DescriptorMatcher::radiusMatch(InputArray queryDescriptors, InputArray trainDescriptors, vector<vector<DMatch>>& matches, float maxDistance, InputArray mask=noArray(), bool compactResult=false)` function also finds the matches for each query descriptor but not farther than the specified distance. The major drawback of this method is that the magnitude of this distance is not normalized, and it depends on the feature extractor and descriptor used.

> In order to get the best results, we recommend that you use matchers along with descriptors of the same type. Although it is possible to mix binary descriptors with float matchers and the other way around, the results might be inaccurate.

Matching the SURF descriptors

SURF descriptors belong to the family of oriented gradients descriptors. They encode statistical knowledge about the geometrical shapes present in the patch (via histograms of oriented gradients/Haar-like features). They are considered as a more efficient substitution for SIFT. They are the best known multiscale feature description approaches, and their accuracy has been widely tested. They have two main drawbacks though:

- They are patented
- They are slower than binary descriptors

There is a common pipeline in every descriptor matching application that uses the components explained earlier in this chapter. It performs the following steps:

1. Compute interest points in both images.
2. Extract descriptors from the two generated interest point sets.
3. Use a matcher to find connections between descriptors.
4. Filter the results to remove bad matches.

The following is the `matchingSURF` example that follows this pipeline:

```
#include <iostream>
#include "opencv2/core/core.hpp"
#include "opencv2/highgui/highgui.hpp"
#include "opencv2/nonfree/nonfree.hpp"

using namespace std;
```

```cpp
using namespace cv;

int main( int argc, char** argv )
{
    Mat img_orig = imread( argv[1],IMREAD_GRAYSCALE);
    Mat img_fragment = imread( argv[2], IMREAD_GRAYSCALE);
    if(img_orig.empty() || img_fragment.empty())
    {
        cerr << " Failed to load images." << endl;
        return -1;
    }

    //Step 1: Detect keypoints using SURF Detector
    vector<KeyPoint> keypoints1, keypoints2;
    Ptr<FeatureDetector> detector = FeatureDetector::create("SURF");

    detector->detect(img_orig, keypoints1);
    detector->detect(img_fragment, keypoints2);

    //Step 2: Compute descriptors using SURF Extractor
    Ptr<DescriptorExtractor> extractor =
      DescriptorExtractor::create("SURF");
    Mat descriptors1, descriptors2;
    extractor->compute(img_orig, keypoints1, descriptors1);
    extractor->compute(img_fragment, keypoints2, descriptors2);

    //Step 3: Match descriptors using a FlannBased Matcher
    Ptr<DescriptorMatcher> matcher =
      DescriptorMatcher::create("FlannBased");
    vector<DMatch> matches12;
    vector<DMatch> matches21;
    vector<DMatch> good_matches;

    matcher->match(descriptors1, descriptors2, matches12);
    matcher->match(descriptors2, descriptors1, matches21);

    //Step 4: Filter results using cross-checking
    for( size_t i = 0; i < matches12.size(); i++ )
    {
        DMatch forward = matches12[i];
        DMatch backward = matches21[forward.trainIdx];
        if( backward.trainIdx == forward.queryIdx )
            good_matches.push_back( forward );
    }

    //Draw the results
    Mat img_result_matches;
    drawMatches(img_orig, keypoints1, img_fragment, keypoints2,
      good_matches, img_result_matches);
    imshow("Matching SURF Descriptors", img_result_matches);
```

```
    waitKey(0);

    return 0;
}
```

The explanation of the code is given as follows. As we described earlier, following the application pipeline implies performing these steps:

1. The first step to be performed is to detect interest points in the input images. In this example, the common interface is used to create a SURF detector with the line `Ptr<FeatureDetector> detector = FeatureDetector::create("SURF")`.

2. After that, the interest points are detected, and a descriptor extractor is created using the common interface `Ptr<DescriptorExtractor> extractor = DescriptorExtractor::create( "SURF")`. The SURF algorithm is also used to compute the descriptors.

3. The next step is to match the descriptors of both images, and for this purpose, a descriptor matcher is created using the common interface, too. The line, `Ptr<DescriptorMatcher> matcher = DescriptorMatcher::create ("FlannBased")`, creates a new matcher based on the Flann algorithm, which is used to match the descriptors in the following way:

   `matcher->match(descriptors1, descriptors2, matches12)`

4. Finally, the results are filtered. Note that two matching sets are computed, as a cross-checking filter is performed afterwards. This filtering only stores the matches that appear in both sets when using the input images as query and train images. In the following screenshot, we can see the difference when a filter is used to discard matches:

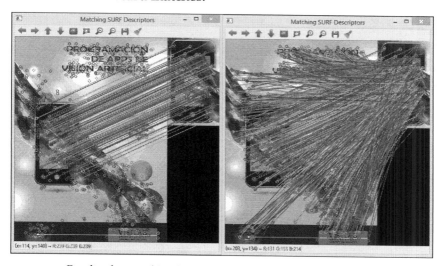

Results after matching SURF descriptors with and without a filter

Matching the AKAZE descriptors

KAZE and AKAZE are novel descriptors included in the upcoming OpenCV 3.0. According to published tests, both outperform the previous detectors included in the library by improving repeatability and distinctiveness for common 2D image-matching applications. AKAZE is much faster than KAZE while obtaining comparable results, so if speed is critical in an application, AKAZE should be used.

The following `matchingAKAZE` example matches descriptors of this novel algorithm:

```cpp
#include <iostream>
#include "opencv2/core/core.hpp"
#include "opencv2/features2d/features2d.hpp"
#include "opencv2/highgui/highgui.hpp"

using namespace cv;
using namespace std;

int main( int argc, char** argv )
{
  Mat img_orig = imread( argv[1], IMREAD_GRAYSCALE );
  Mat img_cam = imread( argv[2], IMREAD_GRAYSCALE );

  if( !img_orig.data || !img_cam.data )
  {
    cerr << " Failed to load images." << endl;
    return -1;
  }

  //Step 1: Detect the keypoints using AKAZE Detector
  Ptr<FeatureDetector> detector = FeatureDetector::create("AKAZE");
  std::vector<KeyPoint> keypoints1, keypoints2;

  detector->detect( img_orig, keypoints1 );
  detector->detect( img_cam, keypoints2 );

  //Step 2: Compute descriptors using AKAZE Extractor
  Ptr<DescriptorExtractor> extractor =
    DescriptorExtractor::create("AKAZE");
  Mat descriptors1, descriptors2;

  extractor->compute( img_orig, keypoints1, descriptors1 );
  extractor->compute( img_cam, keypoints2, descriptors2 );

  //Step 3: Match descriptors using a BruteForce-Hamming Matcher
  Ptr<DescriptorMatcher> matcher =
    DescriptorMatcher::create("BruteForce-Hamming");
```

```
vector<vector<DMatch> > matches;
vector<DMatch> good_matches;

matcher.knnMatch(descriptors1, descriptors2, matches, 2);

//Step 4: Filter results using ratio-test
float ratioT = 0.6;
for(int i = 0; i < (int) matches.size(); i++)
{
    if((matches[i][0].distance <
      ratioT*(matches[i][1].distance)) && ((int)
        matches[i].size()<=2 && (int) matches[i].size()>0))
    {
        good_matches.push_back(matches[i][0]);
    }
}

//Draw the results
Mat img_result_matches;
drawMatches(img_orig, keypoints1, img_cam, keypoints2,
  good_matches, img_result_matches);
imshow("Matching AKAZE Descriptors", img_result_matches);

waitKey(0);

return 0;
}
```

The explanation of the code is given as follows. The first two steps are quite similar to the previous example; the feature detector and descriptor extractor are created through their common interfaces. We only change the string parameter passed to the constructor, as this time, the AKAZE algorithm is used.

 A BruteForce matcher that uses Hamming distance is used this time, as AKAZE is a binary descriptor.

It is created by executing `Ptr<DescriptorMatcher> matcher = DescriptorMatcher ::create("BruteForce-Hamming")`. The `matcher.knnMatch(descriptors1, descriptors2, matches, 2)` function computes the matches between the image descriptors. It is noteworthy to mention the last integer parameter, as it is necessary for the filter processing executed afterwards. This filtering is called Ratio Test, and it computes the goodness of the best match between the goodness of the second best match. To be considered as a good match, this value must be higher than a certain ratio, which can be set in a range of values between 0 and 1. If the ratio tends to be 0, the correspondence between descriptors is stronger.

In the following screenshot, we can see the output when matching a book cover in an image where the book appears rotated:

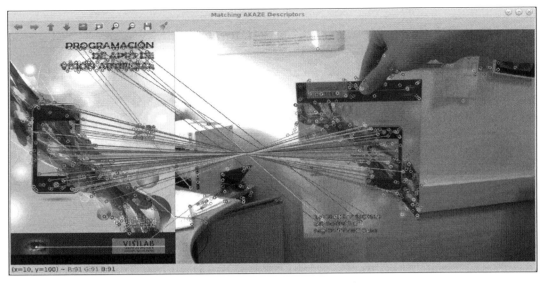

Matching AKAZE descriptors in a rotated image

The following screenshot shows the result when the book does not appear in the second image:

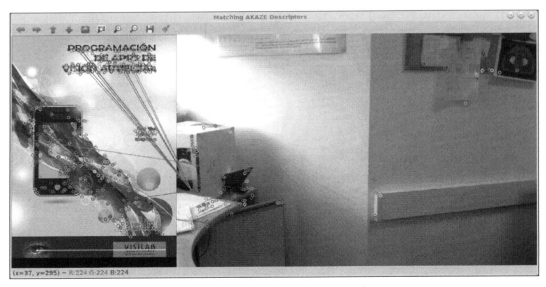

Matching AKAZE descriptors when the train image does not appear

Summary

In this chapter, we have covered a widely used OpenCV component. Local features are a key part of relevant computer vision algorithms such as object recognition, object tracking, image stitching, and camera calibration. An introduction and several samples have been provided, thus covering interest points detection using different algorithms, extraction of descriptors from interest points, matching descriptors, and filtering the results.

What else?

The powerful Bag-of-Words object categorization framework has not been included. This is actually an additional step to what we have covered in this chapter, as extracted descriptors are clustered and used to perform categorization. A complete sample can be found at `[opencv_source_code]/samples/cpp/bagofwords_classification.cpp`.

.

6
Where's Wally? Object Detection

This chapter explains how to use the different options included in the OpenCV object detection module. With the sample code included, it is possible to use Cascade and Latent SVM detectors as well as create custom cascade detectors for a specific object detection application. Additionally, the new Scene Text Detector included in OpenCV 3 is explained in the chapter.

Object detection

Object detection deals with the process of locating instances of a certain class of real-world objects, such as faces, cars, pedestrians, and buildings in images or videos. Detection algorithms typically start by extracting features from two sets of images. One of these sets contains images from the desired object and the other one contains background images where the searched object is not present. Then, the detector is trained based on these features to recognize future instances of the object class.

 Fingerprint recognition, now included in some laptops and smartphones, or face detection, seen in most digital cameras, are everyday examples of object detection applications.

Detecting objects with OpenCV

OpenCV has a number of object detection algorithms implemented in its `objdetect` module. In this module, Cascade and Latent SVM detectors are implemented together with the new Scene Text Detector added in OpenCV 3. All of these algorithms are relatively efficient and obtain accurate results.

Cascades are beautiful

Most objects' detection problems, such as face/person detection or lesion detection in medicine, require searching for the object in many image patches. However, examining all image zones and computing the feature set for each zone are time-consuming tasks. Cascade detectors are widely used because of their high efficiency in doing this.

Cascade detectors consist of various boosting stages. The boosting algorithm selects the best feature set to create and combine a number of weak tree classifiers. Thus, boosting is not only a detector but also a feature selection method. Each stage is usually trained to detect nearly 100 percent of objects correctly and discard at least 50 percent of the background images. Therefore, background images, which represent a larger number of images, need less processing time as they are discarded at the early stages of the cascade. Moreover, the concluding cascade stages use more features than earlier stages, and even then only objects and difficult background images require more time to be evaluated.

Discrete AdaBoost (Adaptive Boosting), Real AdaBoost, Gentle AdaBoost, and LogitBoost are all implemented in OpenCV as boosting stages. On the other hand, it is possible to use Haar-like, **Local Binary Patterns (LBP)** and **Histograms of Oriented Gradients (HOG)** features together with the different boosting algorithms.

All these advantages and available techniques make cascades very useful for building practical detection applications.

Object detection using cascades

OpenCV comes with several pretrained cascade detectors for the most common detection problems. They are located under the OPENCV_SOURCE\data directory. The following is a list of some of them and their corresponding subdirectories:

- Subdirectory haarcascades:
    - haarcascade_frontalface_default.xml
    - haarcascade_eye.xml
    - haarcascade_mcs_nose.xml
    - haarcascade_mcs_mouth.xml
    - haarcascade_upperbody.xml
    - haarcascade_lowerbody.xml
    - haarcascade_fullbody.xml

- Subdirectory `lbpcascades`:
    - ◦ `lbpcascade_frontalface.xml`
    - ◦ `lbpcascade_profileface.xml`
    - ◦ `lbpcascade_silverware.xml`
- Subdirectory `hogcascades`:
    - ◦ `hogcascade_pedestrians.xml`

The following `pedestrianDetection` example serves to illustrate how to use a cascade detector and localize pedestrians in a video file with OpenCV:

```
#include "opencv2/core/core.hpp"
#include "opencv2/objdetect/objdetect.hpp"
#include "opencv2/highgui/highgui.hpp"
#include "opencv2/imgproc/imgproc.hpp"
#include <iostream>

using namespace std;
using namespace cv;

int main(int argc, char *argv[]){
    CascadeClassifier cascade(argv[1]);
    if (cascade.empty())
        return -1;

    VideoCapture vid(argv[2]);
    if (!vid.isOpened()){
        cout<<"Error. The video cannot be opened."<<endl;
        return -1;
    }

    namedWindow("Pedestrian Detection");
    Mat frame;
    while(1) {
        if (!vid.read(frame))
            break;

        Mat frame_gray;
        if(frame.channels()>1){
            cvtColor( frame, frame_gray, CV_BGR2GRAY );
            equalizeHist( frame_gray, frame_gray );
        }else{
            frame_gray = frame;
        }

        vector<Rect> pedestrians;
```

```
cascade.detectMultiScale( frame_gray, pedestrians,
                          1.1, 2, 0, Size(30, 30),
                          Size(150, 150) );

for( size_t i = 0; i < pedestrians.size(); i++ ) {
    Point center( pedestrians[i].x +
                  pedestrians[i].width*0.5,
                  pedestrians[i].y +
                  pedestrians[i].height*0.5 );
    ellipse( frame, center,
             Size( pedestrians[i].width*0.5,
             pedestrians[i].height*0.5), 0, 0, 360,
             Scalar( 255, 0, 255 ), 4, 8, 0 );
}

imshow("Pedestrian Detection", frame);
if(waitKey(100) >= 0)
    break;
}
return 0;
}
```

The code explanation is as follows:

- `CascadeClassifier`: This class provides all the methods needed when working with cascades. An object from this class represents a trained cascade detector.

- constructor `CascadeClassifier:: CascadeClassifier(const string& filename)`: This class initializes the object instance and loads the information of the cascade detector stored in the system file indicated by the variable `filename`.

 Note that the method `bool CascadeClassifier: :load(const string& filename)` is actually called implicitly after the constructor.

- `bool CascadeClassifier:: empty()`: This method checks if a cascade detector has been loaded.

- cvtColor and equalizeHist: These methods are required for image grayscale conversion and equalization. Since the cascade detector is trained with grayscale images and input images can be in different formats, it is necessary to convert them to the correct color space and equalize their histograms in order to obtain better results. This is done by the following code that uses the cvtColor and equalizeHist functions:

```
Mat frame_gray;
if(frame.channels()>1){
    cvtColor( frame, frame_gray, CV_BGR2GRAY );
    equalizeHist( frame_gray, frame_gray );
}else{
    frame_gray = frame;
}
```

- void CascadeClassifier::detectMultiScale(const Mat& image, vector<Rect>& objects, double scaleFactor=1.1, int minNeighbors=3, int flags=0, Size minSize=Size(), Size maxSize=Size()): This method examines the image in the image variable applying the loaded cascade and insert all detected objects in objects. Detections are stored in a vector of rectangles of type Rect. The parameters scaleFactor and minNeighbors indicates how much the image size is reduced at each image scale considered and the minimum number of neighbors that indicate a positive detection. Detections are bound by the minimum and maximum sizes, indicated by minSize and maxSize. Finally, the parameter flags is not used when using cascades created with opencv_traincascade.

 After obtaining the vector that stores the detected objects, it is easy to show them over the original images by reading the coordinates of each rectangle, represented by objects of the class Rect, and drawing a polygon in the indicated zones.

The following screenshot shows the result of applying the `hogcascade_pedestrians.` `xml` pretrained HOG-based pedestrian detector over the frames of the `768x576.avi` video, which is stored in the `OPENCV_SCR/samples` folder.

Pedestrian detection using the OpenCV-trained HOG cascade detector

There are several projects and contributions to the OpenCV community that solve other detection-related problems that involve not only detecting the object but also distinguishing its state. One example of this type of detectors is the smile detector included in OpenCV since Version 2.4.4. The code can be found in the file `OPENCV_SCR/samples/c/smiledetect.cpp`, and the XML that stores the cascade detector, `haarcascade_smile.xml`, can be found in `OPENCV_SCR/data/` `haarcascades`. This code first detects the frontal face using the pretrained cascade stored in `haarcascade_frontalface_alt.xml` and then detects the smiling mouth pattern at the bottom part of the image. Finally, the intensity of the smile is calculated based on the number of neighbors detected.

Training your own cascade

Although OpenCV provides pretrained cascades, in some cases it is necessary to train a cascade detector to look for a specific object. For these cases, OpenCV comes with tools to help train a cascade, generating all the data needed during the training process and the final files with the detector information. These are usually stored in the OPENCV_BUILD\install\x64\mingw\bin directory. Some of the applications are listed as follows:

- opencv_haartraining: This application is historically the first version of the application for creating cascades.

- opencv_traincascade: This application is the latest version of the application for creating cascades.

- opencv_createsamples: This application is used to create the .vec file with the images that contain instances of the object. The file generated is accepted by both the preceding training executables.

- opencv_performance: This application may be used to evaluate a cascade trained with the opencv_haartraining tool. It uses a set of marked images to obtain information about the evaluation, for example, the false alarm or the detection rates.

Since opencv_haartraining is the older version of the program and it comes with fewer features than opencv_traincascade, only the latter will be described here.

Here, the cascade training process is explained using the MIT CBCL face database. This database contains face and background images of 19 x 19 pixels arranged as shown in the following screenshot:

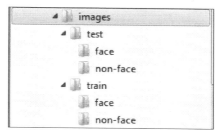

Image file organization

This section explains the training process on Windows. For Linux and Mac OS X, the process is similar but takes into account the specific aspects of the operating system. More information on training cascade detectors in Linux and Mac OS X can be found at `http://opencvuser.blogspot.co.uk/2011/08/creating-haar-cascade-classifier-aka.html` and `http://kaflurbaleen.blogspot.co.uk/2012/11/how-to-train-your-classifier-on-mac.html` respectively.

The training process involves the following steps:

1. **Setting the current directory**: In the **Command Prompt** window, set the current directory to the directory in which training images are stored. For example, if the directory is `C:\chapter6\images`, use the following command:

    ```
    >cd C:\chapter6\images
    ```

2. **Creating the background images information text file**: If background images are stored in `C:\chapter6\images\train\non-face` and their format is `.pgm`, it is possible to create the text file required by OpenCV using the following command:

    ```
    >for %i in (C:\chapter6\images\train\non-face\*.pgm) do @echo %i
    >> train_non-face.txt
    ```

    The following screenshot shows the contents of the background image information file. This file contains the path of the background images:

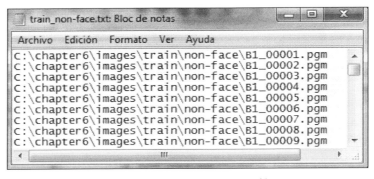

Background images information file

3. **Creating the object images file:** This involves the following two steps:

   1. Creating the `.dat` file with the object coordinates. In this particular database, object images only contain one instance of the object and it is located in the center of the image and scaled to occupy the entire image. Therefore, the number of objects per image is 1 and the object coordinates are `0 0 19 19`, which are the initial point and the width and height of the rectangle that contains the object.

      If object images are stored in `C:\chapter6\images\train\face`, it is possible to use the following command to generate the file:

      ```
      >for %i in (C:\chapter6\images\train\face\*.pgm) do @echo %i
      1 0 0 19 19 >> train_face.dat
      ```

      The content of the `.dat` file can be seen in the following screenshot:

      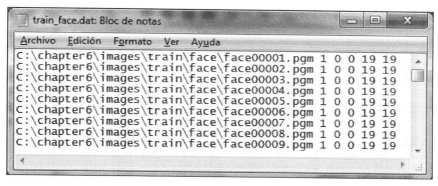

      Object images file

   2. After creating the `.dat` file with the object coordinates, it is necessary to create the `.vec` file that is needed by OpenCV. This step can be performed using the `opencv_createsamples` program with the arguments `-info` (`.dat` file); `-vec` (`.vec` output file name); `-num` (number of images); `-w` and `-h` (output image width and height); and `-maxxangle`, `-maxyangle`, and `-maxzangle` (image rotation angles). To see more options, execute `opencv_createsamples` without arguments. In this case, the command used is:

      ```
      >opencv_createsamples -info train_face.dat -vec train_
      face.vec -num 2429 -w 19 -h 19 -maxxangle 0 -maxyangle 0
      -maxzangle 0
      ```

 OpenCV includes a sample `.vec` file with facial images of size 24 x 24 pixels.

4. **Training the cascade**: Finally, use the `opencv_traincascade` executable and train the cascade detector. The command used in this case is:

```
>opencv_traincascade -data C:\chapter6\trainedCascade -vec
   train_face.vec -bg train_non-face.txt -numPos 242 -numNeg
     454 -numStages 10 -w 19 -h 19
```

The arguments indicate the output directory (`-data`), the `.vec` file (`-vec`), the background information file (`-bg`), the number of positive and negative images to train each stage (`-numPos` and `–numNeg`), the maximum number of stages (`-numStages`), and the width and height of the images (`-w` and `–h`).

The output of the training process is:

```
PARAMETERS:
cascadeDirName: C:\chapter6\trainedCascade
vecFileName: train_face.vec
bgFileName: train_non-face.txt
numPos: 242
numNeg: 454
numStages: 10
precalcValBufSize[Mb] : 256
precalcIdxBufSize[Mb] : 256
stageType: BOOST
featureType: HAAR
sampleWidth: 19
sampleHeight: 19
boostType: GAB
minHitRate: 0.995
maxFalseAlarmRate: 0.5
weightTrimRate: 0.95
maxDepth: 1
maxWeakCount: 100
mode: BASIC
===== TRAINING 0-stage =====
<BEGIN
POS count : consumed    242 : 242
NEG count : acceptanceRatio    454 : 1
```

```
Precalculation time: 4.524
+----+---------+---------+
|  N |    HR   |    FA   |
+----+---------+---------+
|   1|        1|        1|
+----+---------+---------+
|   2|        1|        1|
+----+---------+---------+
|   3| 0.995868| 0.314978|
+----+---------+---------+
END>
Training until now has taken 0 days 0 hours 0 minutes 9 seconds.
. . . Stages 1, 2, 3, and 4 . . .
===== TRAINING 5-stage =====
<BEGIN
POS count : consumed    242 : 247
NEG count : acceptanceRatio    454 : 0.000220059
Required leaf false alarm rate achieved. Branch training
terminated.
```

Finally, the XML files of the cascade are stored in the output directory. These files are `cascade.xml`, `params.xml`, and a set of `stageX.xml` files where X is the stage number.

Latent SVM

Latent SVM is a detector that uses HOG features and a star-structured, part-based model consisting of a root filter and a set of part filters to represent an object category. HOGs are feature descriptors that are obtained by counting the occurrences of gradient orientations in localized portions of an image. On the other hand, a variant of **support vector machines** (**SVM**) classifiers are used in this detector to train models using partially labeled data. The basic idea of an SVM is constructing a hyperplane or set of hyperplanes in high-dimensional space. These hyperplanes are obtained to have the largest distance to the nearest training data point (functional margin in order to achieve low generalization errors). Like cascade detectors, Latent SVM uses a sliding window with different initial positions and scales where the algorithm is applied in order to detect if there is an object inside.

One of the advantages of the OpenCV Latent SVM implementation is that it allows the detection of multiple object categories by combining several simple pretrained detectors within the same multiobject detector instance.

The following `latentDetection` example illustrates how to use a Latent SVM detector for localizing objects from a category in an image:

```cpp
#include "opencv2/core/core.hpp"
#include "opencv2/objdetect/objdetect.hpp"
#include "opencv2/highgui/highgui.hpp"
#include <iostream>

using namespace std;
using namespace cv;

int main(int argc, char* argv[]){
    String model = argv[1];
    vector<String> models;
    models.push_back( model );
    vector<String> names;
    names.push_back( "category" );
    LatentSvmDetector detector( models , names);
    if( detector.empty() ) {
        cout << "Model cannot be loaded" << endl;
        return -1;
    }

    String img = argv[2];
    Mat image = imread( img );
    if( image.empty() ){
        cout << "Image cannot be loaded" << endl;
        return -1;
    }

    vector<LatentSvmDetector::ObjectDetection> detections;
    detector.detect( image, detections, 0.1, 1);
    for( size_t i = 0; i < detections.size(); i++ ) {
        Point center( detections[i].rect.x +
                    detections[i].rect.width*0.5,
                    detections[i].rect.y +
                    detections[i].rect.height*0.5 );
        ellipse( image, center, Size( detections[i].rect.width*0.5,
                detections[i].rect.height*0.5), 0, 0, 360,
                Scalar( 255, 0, 255 ), 4, 8, 0 );
    }
    imshow( "result", image );
    waitKey(0);
    return 0;
}
```

The code explanation is as follows:

- `LatentSvmDetector`: This class has an object that represents a Latent SVM detector composed of one or more pretrained detectors.

- constructor `LatentSvmDetector::LatentSvmDetector(const vector<String>& filenames, const vector<string>& classNames=vector<String>())`: This class initializes the object instance and loads the information of the detectors stored in the system paths indicated by the vector `filenames`. The second parameter, the vector `classNames`, contains the category names. The method `bool LatentSvmDetector::load(const vector<string>& filenames, const vector<string>& classNames=vector<string>())` is called implicitly after the constructor.

- void `LatentSvmDetector::detect(const Mat& image, vector<ObjectDetection>& objectDetections, float overlapThreshold = 0.5f, int numThreads = -1)`: This method examines the image in the variable `image` by applying the simple or combined detector on it and puts all detected objects in `objectDetections`. All detections are stored in a vector of the `ObjectDetection` struct. This structure has the following three variables:

  - The bounding box of the detection (`rect`)
  - The confidence level (`score`)
  - The category ID (`classID`)

  The parameter `overlapThreshold` is the threshold for the non-maximum suppression algorithm for eliminating overlapped detections. Finally, `numThreads` is the number of threads used in the parallel version of the algorithm.

The following screenshot shows a cat detected using the previous code and the files `cat.xml` and `cat.png`, and cars detected using `car.xml` and `cars.png`. These files are included in the OpenCV extra data that can be found in the official repository. Thus, it is possible to run the program using the following command:

```
>latentDetection.exe xmlfile imagefile
```

In the previous command, `xmlfile` is the Latent SVM detector and `imagefile` is the image that has to be examined.

 OpenCV extra data provides more samples and test files that can be used by users to create and test their own projects while saving time. It can be found at `https://github.com/Itseez/opencv_extra`.

In addition to the car and cat detectors, OpenCV provides pretrained detectors for the rest of the classes defined in *The PASCAL Visual Object Classes Challenge 2007* (`http://pascallin.ecs.soton.ac.uk/challenges/VOC/voc2007`). These detectors are as follows:

- `aeroplane.xml`
- `bicycle.xml`
- `bird.xml`
- `boat.xml`
- `bottle.xml`
- `bus.xml`
- `car.xml`
- `cat.xml`
- `chair.xml`
- `cow.xml`
- `diningtable.xml`
- `dog.xml`
- `horse.xml`
- `motorbike.xml`
- `person.xml`
- `pottedplant.xml`
- `sheep.xml`
- `sofa.xml`
- `train.xml`
- `tvmonitor.xml`

The detection of a cat and some cars using Latent SVM

> 💡 The false positive rate can be adjusted by changing the value of the `overlapThreshold` parameter.

Scene text detection

The scene text detection algorithm builds a component tree of an image by thresholding it step-by-step from 0 to 255. To enhance the results, this process is done for each color channel, intensity, and gradient magnitude images. After that, the connected components obtained from successive levels are hierarchically organized depending on their inclusion relationship as shown in the following diagram. This tree organization may contain a huge number of regions:

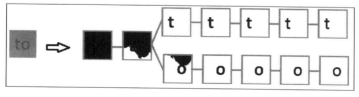

Tree organization example

Thus, the algorithm selects some regions following two stages. Firstly, area, perimeter, bounding box, and Euler number descriptors are computed for each region and used in order to estimate the class-condition probability. External regions with local maximum probabilities are selected if their values are above a global limit and the difference between their local maximum and minimum is also above a specified limit.

The second stage consists of classifying the external regions selected in the first stage into character and non-character classes using whole area ratio, convex hull ratio, and the number of outer boundary inflexion points as features.

Finally, the external regions selected are grouped to obtain words, lines, or paragraphs. This part of the algorithm uses a perceptual-organization-based clustering analysis.

The following `textDetection` example illustrates how to use the Scene Text Detection algorithm and localize text in an image:

```cpp
#include "opencv2/opencv.hpp"
#include "opencv2/objdetect.hpp"
#include "opencv2/highgui.hpp"
#include "opencv2/imgproc.hpp"

#include <vector>
#include <iostream>
#include <iomanip>

using namespace std;
using namespace cv;

int main(int argc, const char * argv[]){

    Mat src = imread(argv[1]);

    vector<Mat> channels;
    computeNMChannels(src, channels);

    //Negative images from RGB channels
    channels.push_back(255-channels[0]);
    channels.push_back(255-channels[1]);
    channels.push_back(255-channels[2]);
    channels.push_back(255-channels[3]);
```

```cpp
for (int c = 0; c < channels.size(); c++){
    stringstream ss;
    ss << "Channel: " << c;
    imshow(ss.str(),channels.at(c));
}

Ptr<ERFilter> er_filter1 = createERFilterNM1(
                            loadClassifierNM1(argv[2]),
                            16, 0.00015f, 0.13f, 0.2f,
                            true, 0.1f );
Ptr<ERFilter> er_filter2 = createERFilterNM2(
                            loadClassifierNM2(argv[3]),
                            0.5 );

vector<vector<ERStat> > regions(channels.size());
// Apply filters to each channel
for (int c=0; c<(int)channels.size(); c++){
    er_filter1->run(channels[c], regions[c]);
    er_filter2->run(channels[c], regions[c]);
}
for (int c=0; c<(int)channels.size(); c++){
    Mat dst = Mat::zeros( channels[0].rows +
                        2, channels[0].cols + 2, CV_8UC1 );
    // Show ERs
    for (int r=0; r<(int)regions[c].size(); r++)
    {
        ERStat er = regions[c][r];
        if (er.parent != NULL){
            int newMaskVal = 255;
            int flags = 4 + (newMaskVal << 8) +
                        FLOODFILL_FIXED_RANGE +
                        FLOODFILL_MASK_ONLY;
            floodFill( channels[c], dst, Point(er.pixel %
                    channels[c].cols,er.pixel /
                    channels[c].cols), Scalar(255), 0,
                    Scalar(er.level), Scalar(0), flags);
        }
    }
    stringstream ss;
    ss << "Regions/Channel: " << c;
    imshow(ss.str(), dst);
```

```
    }

    vector<Rect> groups;
    erGrouping( channels, regions, argv[4], 0.5, groups );
    for (int i=(int)groups.size()-1; i>=0; i--)
    {
        if (src.type() == CV_8UC3)
            rectangle( src,groups.at(i).tl(), groups.at(i).br(),
                       Scalar( 0, 255, 255 ), 3, 8 );
        else
            rectangle( src,groups.at(i).tl(), groups.at(i).br(),
                       Scalar( 255 ), 3, 8 );
    }
    imshow("grouping",src);

    waitKey(-1);
    er_filter1.release();
    er_filter2.release();
    regions.clear();
    groups.clear();
}
```

The code explanation is as follows:

- void computeNMChannels(InputArray _src, OutputArrayOfArrays _channels, int _mode=ERFILTER_NM_RGBLGrad): This function computes different channels from the image in _src to be processed independently in order to obtain high localization recall. These channels are red (R), green (G), blue (B), lightness (L), and gradient magnitude (∇) by default (_mode=ERFILTER_NM_RGBLGrad), it is intensity (I), hue (H), saturation (S), and gradient magnitude (∇) if _mode=ERFILTER_NM_IHSGrad. Finally, the computed channels are saved in the _channels parameter.

- `Ptr<ERFilter> createERFilterNM1(const Ptr<ERFilter::Callback>& cb, int thresholdDelta = 1, float minArea = 0.00025, float maxArea = 0.13, float minProbability = 0.4, bool nonMaxSuppression = true, float minProbabilityDiff = 0.1)`: This function creates an Extremal Region Filter for the classifier of the first stage defined by the algorithm. The first parameter loads the classifier by means of the function `loadClassifierNM1(const std::string& filename)`. The `thresholdDelta` variable indicates the threshold step during the component tree obtaining process. The parameters `minArea` and `maxArea` establish the percentages of the image size between which external regions are retrieved. The value of the `bool` parameter `nonMaxSuppression` is `true` when non-maximum suppression is applied over the branch probabilities, and `false` otherwise. Finally, the `minProbability` and `minProbabilityDiff` parameters control the minimum probability value and the minimum probability difference between local maxima and minima values allowed for retrieving an external region.

- `Ptr<ERFilter> createERFilterNM2(const Ptr<ERFilter::Callback>& cb, float minProbability = 0.3)`: This function creates an External Region Filter for the classifier of the second stage defined by the algorithm. The first parameter loads the classifier by means of the function `loadClassifierNM2(const std::string& filename)`. The other parameter, `minProbability`, is the minimum probability allowed for retrieved external regions.

- `void ERFilter::run( InputArray image, std::vector<ERStat>& regions)`: This method applies the cascade classifier loaded by the filter to obtain the external regions either in the first or the second level. The `image` parameter is the channel that has to be examined and `regions` is a vector with the output of the first stage and also the input/output of the second one.

- `void erGrouping(InputArrayOfArrays src, std::vector<std::vector<ERStat>>& regions, const std::string& filename, float minProbability, std::vector<Rect>& groups)`: This function groups the external regions obtained. It uses the extracted channels (`src`), the obtained external regions by each channel (`regions`), the path to the grouping classifier, and the minimum probability for accepting a group (`minProbability`). Final groups, which are rectangles from `Rect`, are stored in the vector `groups`.

The following group of screenshots shows the obtained image channels. These are red (R), green (G), blue (B), intensity (I), gradient magnitude (∇), inverted red (iR), inverted green (iG), inverted blue (iB), and inverted intensity (iI). In the first row, the R, G, and B channels are shown. The second row shows the I, ∇, and iR channels. Finally, in the third row, the iG, iB, and iI channels are shown:

Extracted image channels

The following group of screenshots shows it is possible to see the external regions extracted from each channel. Channels R, G, B, L, and ∇ produce more accurate results. In the first row, external regions from the R, G, and B channels are shown. The second row shows the external regions extracted from the I, ∇, and iR channels. Finally, in the third row, the iG, iB, and iI channels are shown:

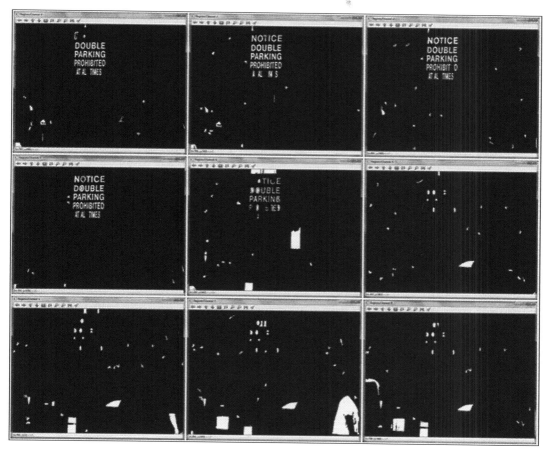

External regions obtained from each channel

Finally, the following screenshot shows the input image with the text areas grouped into lines and paragraphs:

Groups obtained

To reproduce these results or use the OpenCV Scene Text Detector, it is possible to use this code with the sample files provided by the library. The input image and classifier can be found in the OPENCV_SCR/ samples/cpp directory. The image used here is cenetext01.jpg. The first and second level classifiers are trained_classifierNM1.xml and trained_classifierNM2.xml. Finally, the grouping classifier provided by OpenCV is trained_classifier_erGrouping.xml.

Summary

This chapter covers the OpenCV `objdetect` module. It explains how to use and train the Cascade detectors as well as how to use Latent SVM detectors. Moreover, the new Scene Text Detector included in OpenCV 3 has been explained in this chapter.

Methods for detecting and tracking objects in motion are explained in the next chapter.

What else?

Cascade detectors have been widely used in several applications such as face recognition and pedestrian detection because they are fast and provide good results. Soft cascades are a variant of the classic cascade detectors. This new type of cascades is implemented in OpenCV 3 in the `softcascade` module. Soft cascade is trained with AdaBoost but the resulting detector is composed of only one stage. This stage has several weak classifiers that are evaluated in sequence. After evaluating each weak classifier, the result is compared with the corresponding threshold. Similar to the evaluation process carried out in multistage cascades, negative non-object instances are discarded as soon as possible.

What Is He Doing? Motion

7

In this chapter, we will show you different techniques related to motion, as estimated from video frames. After a short introduction and definitions, we will show you how to read video frames captured from a camera. Then, we will tackle the all-important Optical Flow technique. In the third section, we will show you different functions that can be used for tracking. The Motion history and Background subtraction techniques are explained in the fourth and fifth sections, respectively. Finally, image alignment with the ECC method is explained. Every example has been developed and tested for the latest version of OpenCV in GitHub. Most of the functions can work in the previous versions equally, leading to some changes that will be discussed. Most of the functions introduced in this chapter are in the `video` module.

To test the latest source code available in GitHub, go to `https://github.com/itseez/opencv` and download the library code as a ZIP file. Then unzip it to a local folder and follow the same steps described in *Chapter 1, Getting Started*, to compile and install the library.

Motion history

Motion is a very important topic in Computer Vision. Once we detect and isolate an object or person of interest, we can extract valuable data such as positions, velocity, acceleration, and so on. This information can be used for action recognition, behavior pattern studies, video stabilization, augmented reality, and so on.

The Optical Flow technique is a pattern of an object's apparent motion. Surfaces and edges in a visual scene are caused by relative motion between an observer and scene or between the camera and the scene. The concept of the Optical Flow technique is central in Computer Vision and is associated with techniques/tasks such as motion detection, object segmentation, time-to-control information, focus of expansion calculations, luminance, motion compensated encoding, and stereo disparity measurement.

Video tracking consists of locating a moving object (or multiple objects) over time using videos captured from a camera or file. The aim of video tracking is to associate target objects in consecutive video frames. It has a variety of uses, some of which are video editing, medical imaging, traffic control, augmented reality, video communication and compression, security and surveillance, and human-computer interaction.

Motion templates were invented at the MIT Media Lab by Bobick and David in 1996. The use of the motion templates is a simple yet robust technique that tracks general movement. OpenCV motion template functions only work with single channel images. A silhouette (or part of a silhouette) of an object is needed. These silhouettes can be obtained in different ways. For example, segmentation techniques can be used to detect the interest object and then perform tracking with motion templates. Another option is to use the Background subtraction technique to detect foreground objects and then track them. There are other techniques too, although, in this chapter, we will see two examples that use the Background subtraction technique.

Background subtraction is a technique by which an image foreground or region of interest is extracted for further processing, for example, people, cars, text, and so on. The Background subtraction technique is a widely used approach for detecting moving objects in videos captured from static cameras. The essence of the Background subtraction technique is to detect the moving objects from differences between current frames and a reference image taken without target objects present, which is usually called a background image.

Image alignment can be seen as a mapping between the coordinate systems of two or more images taken from different points of view. The first step is, therefore, the choice of an appropriate geometric transformation that adequately models this mapping. This algorithm can be used in a wide range of applications, such as image registration, object tracking, super-resolution, and visual surveillance by moving cameras.

Reading video sequences

To process a video sequence, we should be able to read each frame. OpenCV has developed an easy-to-use framework that can work with video files and camera input.

The following code is a `videoCamera` example that works with a video captured from a video camera. This example is a modification of an example in *Chapter 1, Getting Started*, and we will use it as the basic structure for other examples in this chapter:

```
#include "opencv2/opencv.hpp"

using namespace std;
```

```
using namespace cv;

int videoCamera()
{
    //1-Open the video camera
    VideoCapture capture(0);

    //Check if video camera is opened
    if(!capture.isOpened()) return 1;

    bool finish = false;
    Mat frame;
    Mat prev_frame;
    namedWindow("Video Camera");

    if(!capture.read(prev_frame)) return 1;

    //Convert to gray image
    cvtColor(prev_frame,prev_frame,COLOR_BGR2GRAY);

    while(!finish)
    {
        //2-Read each frame, if possible
        if(!capture.read(frame)) return 1;

        //Convert to gray image
        cvtColor(frame ,frame, COLOR_BGR2GRAY);

        //Here, we will put other functions

        imshow("Video Camera", prev_frame);

        //Press Esc to finish
        if(waitKey(1)==27) finish = true;

        prev_frame = frame;
    }
    //Release the video camera
    capture.release();
    return 0;
}

int main( )
{
    videoCamera();
}
```

The preceding code example creates a window that shows you the grayscale video's camera capture. To initiate the capture, an instance of the `VideoCapture` class has been created with the zero-based camera index. Then, we check whether the video capture can be successfully initiated. Each frame is then read from the video sequence using the `read` method. This video sequence is converted to grayscale using the `cvtColor` method with the `COLOR_BGR2GRAY` parameter and is displayed on the screen until the user presses the *Esc* key. Then, the video sequence is finally released. The previous frame is stored because it will be used for some examples that follow.

> The `COLOR_BGR2GRAY` parameter can be used in OpenCV 3.0. In the previous versions, we also had `CV_BGR2GRAY`.

In the summary, we have shown you a simple method that works with video sequences using a video camera. Most importantly, we have learned how to access each video frame and can now make any type of frame processing.

> With regard to video and audio formats supported by OpenCV, more information can be found at the `ffmpeg.org` website, which presents a complete open source and cross-platform solution for audio and video reading, recording, converting, and streaming. The OpenCV classes that work with video files are built on top of this library. The `Xvid.org` website offers you an open source video codec library based on the MPEG-4 standard for video compression. This codec library has a competitor called DivX, which offers you proprietary but free codec and software tools.

The Lucas-Kanade optical flow

The **Lucas-Kanade** (**LK**) algorithm was originally proposed in 1981, and it has become one of the most successful methods available in Computer Vision. Currently, this method is typically applied to a subset of key points in the input image. This method assumes that optical flow is a necessary constant in a local neighborhood of the pixel that is under consideration and solves the basic Optical Flow technique equations you can see equation (1), for each pixel (x, y) on that neighborhood. The method also assumes that displacements between two consecutive frames are small and are approximately a way to get an over-constrained system of the considered points:

$$I(x, y, t) = I(x + \Delta x, y + \Delta y, t + \Delta t) \qquad (1)$$

We will now focus on the **Pyramidal Lucas-Kanade** method, which estimates the optical flow in a pyramid using the `calcOpticalFlowPyrLK()` function. This method first estimates the optical flow at the top of the pyramid, thus avoiding the problems caused by violations of our assumptions of small and coherent motion. The motion estimate from this first level is then used as the starting point to estimate motion at the next level, as shown in the pyramid in the following diagram:

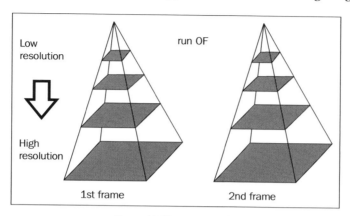

Pyramidal Lucas-Kanade

The following example uses the maxMovement LK function to implement a motion detector:

```
void maxMovementLK(Mat& prev_frame, Mat& frame)
{
    // 1-Detect right features to apply the Optical Flow technique
    vector<Point2f> initial_features;
    goodFeaturesToTrack(prev_frame, initial_features,
        MAX_FEATURES, 0.1, 0.2 );

    // 2-Set the parameters
    vector<Point2f>new_features;
    vector<uchar>status;
    vector<float> err;
    TermCriteria criteria(TermCriteria::COUNT | TermCriteria::EPS,
        20, 0.03);
    Size window(10,10);
    int max_level = 3;
    int flags = 0;
```

```
        double min_eigT = 0.004;

        // 3-Lucas-Kanade method for the Optical Flow technique
        calcOpticalFlowPyrLK(prev_frame, frame, initial_features,
          new_features, status, err, window, max_level, criteria, flags,
            min_eigT );

        // 4-Show the results
        double max_move = 0;
        double movement = 0;
        for(int i=0; i<initial_features.size(); i++)
        {
            Point pointA (initial_features[i].x,
              initial_features[i].y);
            Point pointB(new_features[i].x, new_features[i].y);
            line(prev_frame, pointA, pointB, Scalar(255,0,0), 2);

            movement = norm(pointA-pointB);
            if(movement > max_move)
                max_move = movement;
        }
        if(max_move >MAX_MOVEMENT)
        {
            putText(prev_frame,"INTRUDER",Point(100,100),
              FONT_ITALIC,3,Scalar(255,0,0),5);
            imshow("Video Camera", prev_frame);
            cout << "Press a key to continue..." << endl;
            waitKey();
        }
    }
```

The preceding example shows you a window with each movement. If there is a large movement, a message is displayed on the screen. Firstly, we need to obtain a set of appropriate key points in the image on which we can estimate the optical flow. The goodFeaturesToTrack() function uses the method that was originally proposed by Shi and Tomasi to solve this problem in a reliable way, although you can also use other functions to detect important and easy-to-track features (see *Chapter 5, Focusing on the Interesting 2D Features*). MAX_FEATURES is set to 500 to limit the number of key points. The Lucas-Kanade method parameters are then set and calcOpticalFlowPyrLK() is called. When the function returns, the status (status) array is checked to see which points were successfully tracked and that the new set of points (new_features) with the estimated positions is used. Lines are drawn to represent the motion, and if there is a displacement greater than MAX_MOVEMENT—for example—100, a message is shown on the screen. We can see two screen captures, as follows:

Output of the maxMovementLK example

Using the modified `videoCamera` example, we have applied the `maxMovementLK()` function to detect large movements:

```
...
while(!finish)
{
    capture.read(frame);

    cvtColor(frame,frame,COLOR_BGR2GRAY);

// Detect Maximum Movement with Lucas-Kanade Method
    maxMovementLK(prev_frame, frame);
...
```

This method is computationally efficient because tracking is only performed on important or interesting points.

The Gunnar-Farneback optical flow

The **Gunnar-Farneback** algorithm was developed to produce dense Optical Flow technique results (that is, on a dense grid of points). The first step is to approximate each neighborhood of both frames by quadratic polynomials. Afterwards, considering these quadratic polynomials, a new signal is constructed by a global displacement. Finally, this global displacement is calculated by equating the coefficients in the quadratic polynomials' yields.

Let's now see the implementation of this method, which uses the calcOpticalFlowFarneback() function. The following is an example (maxMovementFarneback) that uses this function to detect the maximum movement as shown in the previous example:

```
void maxMovementFarneback(Mat& prev_frame, Mat& frame)
{
    // 1-Set the Parameters
    Mat optical_flow = Mat(prev_frame.size(), COLOR_BGR2GRAY);
    double pyr_scale = 0.5;
    int levels = 3;
    int win_size = 5;
    int iterations = 5;
    int poly_n = 5;
    double poly_sigma = 1.1;
    int flags = 0;

    // 2-Farneback method for the Optical Flow technique
    calcOpticalFlowFarneback(prev_frame, frame, optical_flow,
      pyr_scale, levels, win_size, iterations, poly_n, poly_sigma,
        flags);

    // 3-Show the movements
    int max_move = 0;
    for (int i = 1; i <optical_flow.rows ; i++)
    {
        for (int j = 1; j <optical_flow.cols ; j++)
        {
            Point2f &p = optical_flow.at<Point2f>(i, j);
            Point pA = Point(round(i + p.x),round(j + p.y));
            Point pB = Point(i, j);
            int move = sqrt(p.x*p.x + p.y*p.y);
            if( move >MIN_MOVEMENT )
            {
                line(prev_frame, pA, pB, Scalar(255,0,0),2);
                if ( move > max_move )
                    max_move = move;
            }
        }
    }
    if(max_move >MAX_MOVEMENT)
    {
        putText(prev_frame,"INTRUDER",Point(100,100),
            FONT_ITALIC,3,Scalar(255,0,0),5);
        imshow("Video Camera", prev_frame);
        cout << "Press a key to continue..." << endl;
        waitKey();
    }
}
```

This function receives two consecutive frames, estimates the optical flow with different parameters, and returns an array with the same size as the input frame, where each pixel is actually a point (Point2f) that represents the displacement for that pixel. Firstly, different parameters are set for this function. Of course, you can also use your own criteria to configure the performance. Then, with these parameters, the Optical Flow technique is performed between each two consecutive frames. Consequently, we obtain an array with the estimations for each pixel, which is optical_flow. Finally, the movements that are greater than MIN_MOVEMENT are displayed on the screen. If the largest movement is greater than MAX_MOVEMENT, then an INTRUDER message is displayed.

Understandably, this method is quite slow because the Optical Flow technique is computed over each pixel on the frame. The output of this algorithm is similar to the previous method, although it's much slower.

The Mean-Shift tracker

The **Mean-Shift** method allows you to locate the maximum of a density function given discrete data sampled from that function. It is, therefore, useful for detecting the modes of this density. Mean-Shift is an iterative method, and an initial estimation is needed.

The algorithm can be used for visual tracking. In this case, the color histogram of the tracked object is used to compute the confidence map. The simplest of such algorithm would create a confidence map in the new image based on the object histogram taken from the previous image, and Mean-Shift is used to find the peak of the confidence map near the object's previous position. The confidence map is a probability density function on the new image, assigning each pixel of the new image a probability, which is the probability of the pixel color occurring in the object in the previous image. Next, we show you an example (trackingMeanShift) using this function:

```
void trackingMeanShift(Mat& img, Rect search_window)
{
    // 1-Criteria to MeanShift function
    TermCriteria criteria(TermCriteria::COUNT | TermCriteria::EPS, 10,
1);

    // 2-Tracking using MeanShift
meanShift(img, search_window, criteria);

    // 3-Show the result
    rectangle(img, search_window, Scalar(0,255,0), 3);
}
```

This example shows you a window with an initial centered rectangle where the tracking is performed. First, the criteria parameter is set. The function that implements the method needs three parameters: the main image, the interest area that we want to search, and the term criteria for different modes of tracking. Finally, a rectangle is obtained from `meanShift()`, and `search_window` is drawn on the main image.

Using a modified `videoCamera` example, we apply this method for tracking. A static window of the screen is used to search. Of course, you can manually adjust another window or use other functions to detect interest objects and then perform the tracking on them:

```
...
while(!finish)
{
    capture.read(frame);

    cvtColor(frame,frame,COLOR_BGR2GRAY);

// Tracking using MeanShift with an initial search window
    Rect search_window(200,150,100,100);
    trackingMeanShift(prev_frame, search_window);
...
```

Here, we can see the following two screen captures:

Output of the trackingMeanShift example

The CamShift tracker

The `CamShift` (**Continuously Adaptive Mean Shift**) algorithm is an image segmentation method that was introduced by Gary Bradski of OpenCV fame in 1998. It differs from `MeanShift` in that a search window adjusts itself in size. If we have a well-segmented distribution (for example, face features that stay compact), this method will automatically adjust itself to the face sizes as the person moves closer or farther from the camera.

> We can find a `CamShift` reference at `http://docs.opencv.org/ trunk/doc/py_tutorials/py_video/py_meanshift/py_ meanshift.html`.

We will now see the following example (`trackingCamShift`) using this method:

```
void trackingCamShift(Mat& img, Rect search_window)
{
    //1-Criteria to CamShift function
    TermCriteria criteria(TermCriteria::COUNT | TermCriteria::EPS,
        10, 1);

    //2-Tracking using CamShift
    RotatedRect found_object = CamShift(img, search_window,
        criteria);

    //3-Bounding rectangle and show the result
    Rect found_rect = found_object.boundingRect();
    rectangle(img, found_rect, Scalar(0,255,0),3);
}
```

This function structure is very similar to the one in the preceding section; the only difference is that a bounding rectangle is returned from `CamShift()`.

The Motion templates

Motion template is a technique in image processing for finding a small part of an image or silhouette that matches a template image. This template matcher is used to make comparisons with respect to similarity and to examine the likeness or difference. Templates might potentially require sampling of a large number of points. However, it is possible to reduce these numbers of points by reducing the resolution of the search; another technique to improve these templates is to use pyramid images.

In OpenCV's examples (`[opencv_source_code]/samples/c/motempl.c`), a related program can be found.

The Motion history template

We now assume that we have a good silhouette or template. New silhouettes are then captured and overlaid using the current time stamp as the weight. These sequentially fading silhouettes record the history of the previous movement and are thus referred to as the Motion history template. Silhouettes whose time stamp is more than a specified DURATION older than the current time stamp are set to zero. We have created a simple example (motionHistory) using the updateMotionHistory() OpenCV function on two frames as follows:

```
void updateMotionHistoryTemplate(Mat& prev_frame, Mat& frame, Mat&
  history)
{
    //1-Calculate the silhouette of difference between the two
    //frames
    absdiff(frame, prev_frame, prev_frame);

    //2-Applying a threshold on the difference image
    double threshold_val = 100;
      threshold(prev_frame,prev_frame,threshold_val,255,
        THRESH_BINARY);

    //3-Calculate the current time
    clock_t aux_time = clock();
    double current_time = (aux_time-INITIAL_TIME)/CLOCKS_PER_SEC;

    //4-Performing the Update Motion history template
    updateMotionHistory(prev_frame, history, current_time,
      DURATION);
}
```

 The THRESH_BINARY parameter can be used on OpenCV 3.0. In the previous versions, we also had CV_THRESH_BINARY.

This example shows you a window where the motion history is drawn. The first step is to obtain a silhouette; the Background subtraction technique is used for this. The difference in the absolute value is obtained from the two input frames. In the second step, a binary thresholding is applied to remove noise from the silhouette. Then, the current time is obtained. The final step is to perform the updating of the Motion history template using OpenCV's function.

We have also set DURATION to 5. Note that it is necessary to initialize INITIAL_TIME and history. Besides, we can use this function call from the modified videoCamera example as follows:

```
...
// Calculate the initial time
INITIAL_TIME = clock()/CLOCKS_PER_SEC;

//Create a Mat to save the Motion history template
Mat history(prev_frame.rows, prev_frame.cols, CV_32FC1);
while(!finish)
{
  capture.read(frame);

  cvtColor(frame,frame,COLOR_BGR2GRAY);

// Using Update Motion history template
  updateMotionHistoryTemplate(prev_frame, frame, history);

  imshow("Video Camera", history);
...
```

To use the clock() function, which gets the current time, we need to include <ctime>. Some screen captures will be shown in which a person is walking in front of the camera.

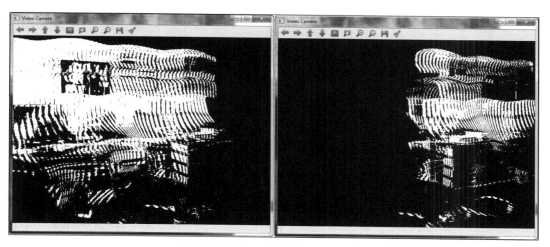

Output of the motionHistory example

The Motion gradient

Once the Motion templates have a collection of object silhouettes overlaid in time, we can obtain the directions of movement by computing the gradients of the history image. The following example (motionGradient) computes the gradients:

```
void motionGradientMethod(Mat& history, Mat& orientations)
{
    //1-Set the parameters
    double max_gradient = 3.0;
    double min_gradient = 1.0;
    //The default 3x3 Sobel filter
    int apertura_size = 3;
    //Distance to show the results
    int dist = 20;
    Mat mask = Mat::ones(history.rows, history.cols, CV_8UC1);

    //2-Calcule motion gradients
    calcMotionGradient(history, mask, orientations, max_gradient,
        min_gradient, apertura_size);

    //3-Show the results
    Mat result = Mat::zeros(orientations.rows, orientations.cols,
        CV_32FC1);
    for (int i=0;i<orientations.rows; i++)
    {
        for (int j=0;j<orientations.cols; j++)
        {
            double angle = 360-orientations.at<float>(i,j);
            if (angle!=360)
            {
                Point point_a(j, i);
                Point point_b(round(j+ cos(angle)*dist), round(i+
                    sin(angle)*dist));
                line(result, point_a, point_b, Scalar(255,0,0),
                    1);
            }
        }
    }
    imshow("Result", result);
}
```

A screen capture is shown with a person moving his head in front of the camera (see the following screenshot). Each line represents the gradient for each pixel. Different frames also overlap at a t time:

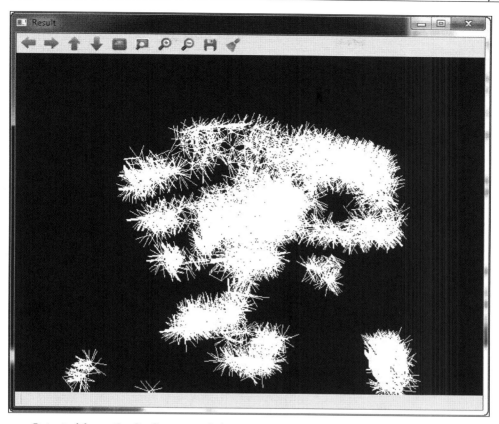

Output of the motionGradient example (a person is moving his head in front of the camera).

The preceding example shows you a window that displays the directions of movement. As the first step, the parameters are set (the maximum and minimum gradient value to be detected). The second step uses the `calcMotionGradient()` function to obtain a matrix of the gradient direction angles. Finally, to show the results, these angles are drawn on the screen using a default distance, which is `dist`. Again, we can use this function from the following modified `videoCamera` example:

```
...
//Create a Mat to save the Motion history template
Mat history(prev_frame.rows, prev_frame.cols, CV_32FC1);
while(!finish)
{
    capture.read(frame);

    cvtColor(frame,frame,COLOR_BGR2GRAY);

//Using Update Motion history template
```

```
    updateMotionHistoryTemplate(prev_frame, frame, history);

//Calculate motion gradients
Mat orientations = Mat::ones(history.rows, history.cols,
    CV_32FC1);
motionGradientMethod(history, orientations);
...
```

The Background subtraction technique

The Background subtraction technique consists of obtaining the important objects over a background.

Now, let's see the methods available in OpenCV for the Background subtraction technique. Currently, the following four important techniques are required for this task:

- **MOG (Mixture-of-Gaussian)**
- **MOG2**
- **GMG (Geometric MultiGrip)**
- **KNN (K-Nearest Neighbors)**

Next, we are going to see an example (backgroundSubKNN) using the KNN technique:

```
#include<opencv2/opencv.hpp>

using namespace cv;
using namespace std;

int backGroundSubKNN()
{
    //1-Set the parameters and initializations
    Mat frame;
    Mat background;
    Mat foreground;
    bool finish = false;
    int history = 500;
    double dist2Threshold = 400.0;
    bool detectShadows = false;
    vector< vector<Point>> contours;
    namedWindow("Frame");
    namedWindow("Background");
    VideoCapture capture(0);

    //Check if the video camera is opened
```

```
        if(!capture.isOpened()) return 1;

        //2-Create the background subtractor KNN
        Ptr <BackgroundSubtractorKNN> bgKNN =
          createBackgroundSubtractorKNN (history, dist2Threshold,
            detectShadows);

        while(!finish)
        {
            //3-Read every frame if possible
            if(!capture.read(frame)) return 1;

            //4-Using apply and getBackgroundImage method to get
            //foreground and background from this frame
            bgKNN->apply(frame, foreground);
            bgKNN->getBackgroundImage(background);

            //5-Reduce the foreground noise
            erode(foreground, foreground, Mat());
            dilate(foreground, foreground, Mat());

            //6-Find the foreground contours
            findContours(foreground,contours,RETR_EXTERNAL,
              CHAIN_APPROX_NONE);
            drawContours(frame,contours,-1,Scalar(0,0,255),2);

            //7-Show the results
            imshow("Frame", frame);
            imshow("Background", background);
            moveWindow("Frame", 0, 100);
            moveWindow("Background",800, 100);

            //Press Esc to finish
            if(waitKey(1) == 27) finish = true;
        }
        capture.release();
        return 0;
}

int main()
{
    backGroundSubKNN();
}
```

 The createBackgroundSubtractorKNN method has only
been included in Version 3.0 of OpenCV.

The Background subtracted frame and screen capture are shown in the following screenshot in which a person is walking in front of the camera:

Output of the backgroundSubKNN example

The preceding example shows you two windows with the subtracted background images and draws contours of the person found. First, parameters are set as the distance threshold between background and each frame to detect objects (dist2Threshol) and the disabling of the shadow detection (detectShadows). In the second step, using the createBackgroundSubtractorKNN() function, a background subtractor is created and a smart pointer construct is used (Ptr<>) so that we will not have to release it. The third step is to read each frame, if possible. Using the apply() and getBackgroundImage() methods, the foreground and background images are obtained. The fifth step is to reduce the foreground noise by applying a morphological closing operation (in the erosion — erode() — and dilation — dilate() — order). Then, contours are detected on the foreground image and then they're drawn. Finally, the background and current frame image are shown.

Image alignment

OpenCV now implements the ECC algorithm, which is only available as of Version 3.0. This method estimates the geometric transformation (warp) between the input and template frames and returns the warped input frame, which must be close to the first template. The estimated transformation is the one that maximizes the correlation coefficient between the template and the warped input frame. In the OpenCV examples ([opencv_source_code]/samples/cpp/image_alignment.cpp), a related program can be found.

The ECC algorithm is based on the ECC criterion of the paper *Parametric Image Alignment Using Enhanced Correlation Coefficient Maximization*. You can find this at http://xanthippi.ceid.upatras.gr/people/evangelidis/george_files/PAMI_2008.pdf.

We are now going to see an example (findCameraMovement) that uses this ECC technique using the findTransformECC() function:

```cpp
#include <opencv2/opencv.hpp>

using namespace cv;
using namespace std;

int findCameraMovement()
{
    //1-Set the parameters and initializations
    bool finish = false;
    Mat frame;
    Mat initial_frame;
    Mat warp_matrix;
    Mat warped_frame;
    int warp_mode = MOTION_HOMOGRAPHY;
    TermCriteria criteria(TermCriteria::COUNT | TermCriteria::EPS,
        50, 0.001);
    VideoCapture capture(0);
    Rect rec(100,50,350,350);    //Initial rectangle
    Mat aux_initial_frame;
    bool follow = false;

    //Check if video camera is opened
    if(!capture.isOpened()) return 1;

    //2-Initial capture
    cout << "\n Press 'c' key to continue..." << endl;
    while(!follow)
    {
        if(!capture.read(initial_frame)) return 1;
        cvtColor(initial_frame ,initial_frame, COLOR_BGR2GRAY);
        aux_initial_frame = initial_frame.clone();
        rectangle(aux_initial_frame, rec, Scalar(255,255,255),3);
        imshow("Initial frame", aux_initial_frame);
        if (waitKey(1) == 99) follow = true;
    }
    Mat template_frame(rec.width,rec.height,CV_32F);
    template_frame = initial_frame.colRange(rec.x, rec.x +
        rec.width).rowRange(rec.y, rec.y + rec.height);
```

```
        imshow("Template image", template_frame);

        while(!finish)
        {
            cout << "\n Press a key to continue..." << endl;
            waitKey();

    warp_matrix = Mat::eye(3, 3, CV_32F);

            //3-Read each frame, if possible
            if(!capture.read(frame)) return 1;

            //Convert to gray image
            cvtColor(frame ,frame, COLOR_BGR2GRAY);

            try
            {
                //4-Use findTransformECC function
                findTransformECC(template_frame, frame, warp_matrix,
                    warp_mode, criteria);

                //5-Obtain the new perspective
                warped_frame = Mat(template_frame.rows,
                    template_frame.cols, CV_32F);
                warpPerspective (frame, warped_frame, warp_matrix,
                    warped_frame.size(), WARP_INVERSE_MAP +
                        WARP_FILL_OUTLIERS);
            }
            catch(Exception e) { cout << "Exception: " << e.err <<
                endl;}

            imshow ("Frame", frame);
            imshow ("Warped frame", warped_frame);

            //Press Esc to finish
            if(waitKey(1) == 27) finish = true;
        }
        capture.release();
        return 0;
    }

    main()
    {
        findCameraMovement();
    }
```

Some screen captures are shown in the following screenshot. The left-column frames represent the initial and template frames. The upper-right image is the current frame and the lower-right image is the warped frame.

Output of the findCameraMovement example.

The code example shows you four windows: the initial template, the initial frame, the current frame, and the warped frame. The first step is to set the initial parameters as `warp_mode` (MOTION_HOMOGRAPHY). The second step is to check whether the video camera is opened and to obtain a template, which will be calculated using a centered rectangle. When the *C* key is pressed, this area will be captured as the template. The third step is to read the next frame and convert it to a gray frame. The `findTransformECC()` function is applied to calculate `warp_matrix` with this matrix, and using `warpPerspective()`, the camera movement can be corrected using `warped_frame`.

Summary

This chapter covered an important subject in Computer Vision. Motion detection is an essential task, and in this chapter, we have provided the reader with the insight and samples that are required for the most useful methods available in OpenCV: working with video sequences (see the videoCamera example), the Optical Flow technique (see the maxMovementLK and maxMovementFarneback examples), tracking (see the trackingMeanShift and trackingCamShift examples), the Motion templates (see the motionHistory and motionGradient examples), the Background subtraction technique (see the backgroundSubKNN example), and image alignment (see the findCameraMovement example).

What else?

Within the OpenCV libraries, there are other functions that deal with motion. Other Optical Flow technique methods are implemented, such as the Horn and Schunk (cvCalcOpticalFlowHS), block machine (cvCalcOpticalFlowBM), and simple flow (calcOpticalFlowSF) methods. A method to estimate the global movement is also available (calcGlobalOrientation). Finally, there are other methods to obtain backgrounds such as MOG (createBackgroundSubtractorMOG), MOG2 (createBackgroundSubtractorMOG2), and GMG (createBackgroundSubtractorGMG) methods.

8

Advanced Topics

This chapter covers the less commonly used topics, such as machine learning with multiple classes and GPU-based optimizations. Both the topics are seeing a growth in interest and practical applications, so they deserve a complete chapter. We consider them advanced only as long as additional knowledge is required about machine learning / statistical classification and parallelization. We will start by explaining some of the most well-known classifiers such as KNN, SVM, and Random Forests, all of which are available in the `ml` module and show how they work with different database formats and multiple classes. Finally, a set of classes and functions to utilize GPU-based computational resources will be described.

Machine learning

Machine learning deals with techniques that allow computers to learn and make decisions by themselves. A central concept in machine learning is the classifier. A classifier learns from the examples in a dataset, where the label of each sample is known. Usually, we have two datasets at hand: training and test. The classifier builds a model using the training set. This trained classifier is expected to predict the label of new unseen samples, so we finally use the test set to validate it and assess label recognition rates.

In this section, we explain the different classes and functions that OpenCV provides for classification, and simple examples of their use. Machine learning classes and functions for statistical classification, regression, and clustering of data are all included in the `ml` module.

The KNN classifier

K-nearest neighbors (KNN) is one of the simplest classifiers. It is a supervised classification method, which learns from available cases and classifies new cases by a minimum distance. K is the number of neighbors to be analyzed in the decision. The new data point to classify (the query) is projected to the same space as the learning points, and its class is given by the most frequent class among its KNN from the training set.

The following KNNClassifier code is an example of using the KNN algorithm to classify each image pixel to the nearest color: black (0, 0, 0), white (255, 255, 255), blue (255, 0, 0), green (0, 255, 0), or red (0, 0, 255):

```cpp
#include <iostream>
#include <opencv2/core/core.hpp>
#include <opencv2/highgui/highgui.hpp>
#include <opencv2/ml/ml.hpp>

using namespace std;
using namespace cv;

int main(int argc, char *argv[]){

//Create Mat for the training set and classes
    Mat classes(5, 1, CV_32FC1);
    Mat colors(5, 3, CV_32FC1);

    //Training set (primary colors)
    colors.at<float>(0,0)=0, colors.at<float>(0,1)=0,
      colors.at<float>(0,2)=0;
    colors.at<float>(1,0)=255, colors.at<float>(1,1)=255,
      colors.at<float>(1,2)=255;
    colors.at<float>(2,0)=255, colors.at<float>(2,1)=0,
      colors.at<float>(2,2)=0;
    colors.at<float>(3,0)=0, colors.at<float>(3,1)=255,
      colors.at<float>(3,2)=0;
    colors.at<float>(4,0)=0, colors.at<float>(4,1)=0,
      colors.at<float>(4,2)=255;

    //Set classes to each training sample
    classes.at<float>(0,0)=1;
    classes.at<float>(1,0)=2;
    classes.at<float>(2,0)=3;
    classes.at<float>(3,0)=4;
    classes.at<float>(4,0)=5;

    //KNN classifier (k=1)
    CvKNearest classifier;
```

```
classifier.train(colors,classes,Mat(),false,1,false);

//Load original image
Mat src=imread("baboon.jpg",1);
imshow("baboon",src);

//Create result image
Mat dst(src.rows , src.cols, CV_8UC3);

Mat results;
Mat newPoint(1,3,CV_32FC1);

//Response for each pixel and store the result in the result
  image
float prediction=0;
for(int y = 0; y < src.rows; ++y){
  for(int x = 0; x < src.cols; ++x){
    newPoint.at<float>(0,0)= src.at<Vec3b>(y, x)[0];
    newPoint.at<float>(0,1) = src.at<Vec3b>(y, x)[1];
    newPoint.at<float>(0,2) = src.at<Vec3b>(y, x)[2];
    prediction=classifier.find_nearest(newPoint,1,&results, 0,
      0);
    dst.at<Vec3b>(y, x)[0]= colors.at<float>(prediction-1,0);
    dst.at<Vec3b>(y, x)[1]= colors.at<float>(prediction-1,1);
    dst.at<Vec3b>(y, x)[2]= colors.at<float>(prediction-1,2);
  }
}

//Show result image
cv::imshow("result KNN",dst);
cv::waitKey(0);
return 0;
}
```

 Remember that OpenCV uses a BGR color scheme.

OpenCV provides the KNN algorithm through the `CvKNearest` class. The training information is added to the KNN classifier through the `bool CvKNearest::train(const Mat& trainData, const Mat& responses, const Mat& sampleIdx, bool isRegression, int maxK, bool updateBase)` function. The example creates a training set with five samples, (`Mat colors(5, 3, CV_32FC1)`), which represent each class (color) (`Mat classes(5, 1, CV_32FC1)`); these are the first two input parameters. The `isRegression` is parameter is a Boolean value that defines whether we want to perform a classification or a regression. The `maxK` value indicates the maximum number of neighbors that will be used in the test phase.

Finally, `updateBaseparameter` allows us to indicate whether we want to train a new classifier with the data or use it to update the previous training data. Then, the code sample performs the test phase with each pixel of the original image using the `float CvKNearest::find_nearest(const Mat& samples, int k, Mat* results=0, const float** neighbors=0, Mat* neighborResponses=0, Mat* dist=0)` function. The function tests the input sample, selecting the KNN, and finally predicts the class value for this sample.

In the following screenshot, we can see the code output and the difference between the original and the result images after this KNN classification:

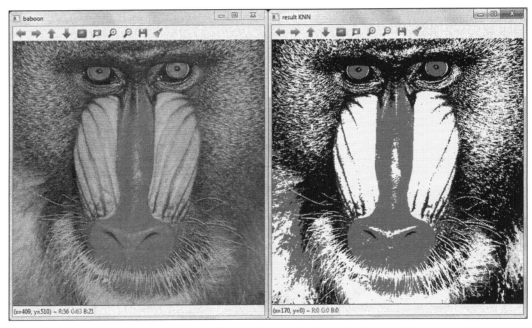

KNN classification using the primary colors as classes (left: the original image, right: the result image)

The Random Forest classifier

Random Forests are a general class of ensemble building methods that use a decision tree as the base classifier. The Random Forest classifier is a variation of the Bagging classifier (Bootstrap Aggregating). The Bagging algorithm is a method of classification that generates weak individual classifiers using bootstrap. Each classifier is trained on a random redistribution of the training set so that many of the original examples may be repeated in each classification.

The principal difference between Bagging and Random Forest is that Bagging uses all the features in each tree node and Random Forest selects a random subset of the features. The suitable number of randomized features corresponds to the square root of the total number of features. For prediction, a new sample is pushed down the tree and it is assigned the class of the terminal (or leaf) node in the tree. This method is iterated over all the trees, and finally, the average vote of all the tree predictions is considered as the prediction result. The following diagram shows the Random Forest algorithm:

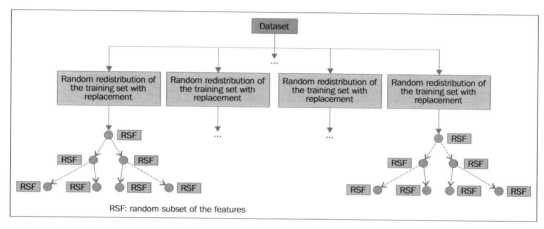

The RF classifier

Random Forests are currently one of the best classifiers available, both in recognition power and efficiency. In our example `RFClassifier`, we use the OpenCV Random Forest classifier and also the OpenCV `CvMLData` class. A large amount of information is typically handled in machine learning problems, and for this reason, it is convenient to use a `.cvs` file. The `CvMLData` class is used to load the training set information from such a file as follows:

```
//… (omitted for simplicity)

int main(int argc, char *argv[]){

    CvMLData mlData;
    mlData.read_csv("iris.csv");
    mlData.set_response_idx(4);
    //Select 75% samples as training set and 25% as test set
    CvTrainTestSplit cvtts(0.75f, true);
    //Split the iris dataset
    mlData.set_train_test_split(&cvtts);

    //Get training set
```

```
Mat trainsindex= mlData.get_train_sample_idx();
cout<<"Number of samples in the training
    set:"<<trainsindex.cols<<endl;
//Get test set
Mat testindex=mlData.get_test_sample_idx();
cout<<"Number of samples in the test
    set:"<<testindex.cols<<endl;
cout<<endl;

//Random Forest parameters
CvRTParams params = CvRTParams(3, 1, 0, false, 2, 0, false, 0,
    100, 0, CV_TERMCRIT_ITER | CV_TERMCRIT_EPS);

CvRTrees classifierRF;
//Taining phase
classifierRF.train(&mlData,params);
std::vector<float> train_responses, test_responses;

//Calculate train error
cout<<"Error on train samples:"<<endl;
cout<<(float)classifierRF.calc_error( &mlData,
    CV_TRAIN_ERROR,&train_responses)<<endl;

//Print train responses
cout<<"Train responses:"<<endl;
for(int i=0;i<(int)train_responses.size();i++)
    cout<<i+1<<":"<<(float)train_responses.at(i)<<"   ";
cout<<endl<<endl;

//Calculate test error
cout<<"Error on test samples:"<<endl;
cout<<(float)classifierRF.calc_error( &mlData,
    CV_TEST_ERROR,&test_responses)<<endl;

//Print test responses
cout<<"Test responses:"<<endl;
for(int i=0;i<(int)test_responses.size();i++)
    cout<<i+1<<":"<<(float)test_responses.at(i)<<"   ";
cout<<endl<<endl;

return 0;
}
```

The dataset has been provided by the UC Irvine Machine Learning Repository, available at http://archive.ics.uci.edu/ml/. For this code sample, the Iris dataset was used.

As we mentioned previously, the CvMLData class allows you to load the dataset from a .csv file using the read_csv function and indicates the class column by the set_response_idx function. In this case, we use this dataset to perform the training and test phases. It is possible to split the dataset into two disjoint sets for training and test. For this, we use the CvTrainTestSplit struct and the void CvMLData::set_train_test_split(const CvTrainTestSplit* spl) function. In the CvTrainTestSplit struct, we indicate the percentage of samples to be used as the training set (0.75 percent in our case) and whether we want to mix the indices of the training and test samples from the dataset. The set_train_test_split function performs the split. Then, we can store each set in Mat with the get_train_sample_idx() and get_test_sample_idx() functions.

The Random Forest classifier is created using the CvRTrees class, and its parameters are defined by the CvRTParams::CvRTParams(int max_depth, int min_sample_count, float regression_accuracy, bool use_surrogates, int max_categories, const float* priors, bool calc_var_importance, int nactive_vars, int max_num_of_trees_in_the_forest, float forest_accuracy, int termcrit_type) constructor. Some of the most important input parameters refer to the maximum depth of the trees (max_depth)—in our sample, it has a value of 3—the number of randomized features in each node (nactive_vars), and the maximum number of trees in the forest (max_num_of_trees_in_the_forest). If we set the nactive_vars parameter to 0, the number of randomized features will be the square root of the total number of features.

Finally, once the classifier is trained with the train function, we can obtain the percentage of misclassified samples using the float CvRTrees::calc_error(CvMLData* data, int type, std::vector<float>* resp=0) method. The parameter type allows you to select the source of the error: CV_TRAIN_ERROR (an error in the training samples) or CV_TEST_ERROR (an error in the test samples).

The following screenshot shows the training and test errors and the classifier responses in both the sets:

The RF classifier sample results

SVM for classification

The **Support Vector Machine** (**SVM**) classifier finds a discriminant function by maximizing the geometrical margin between the classes. Thus, the space is mapped in such a way that the classes are as widely separated as possible. SVM minimizes both the training error and the geometrical margin. Nowadays, this classifier is one of the best classifiers available and has been applied to many real-world problems. The following SVMClassifier sample code performs a classification using the SVM classifier and a dataset of 66 image objects. The dataset is divided into four classes: a training shoe (class 1), a cuddly toy (class 2), a plastic cup (class 3), and a bow (class 4). The following screenshot shows the examples of the four classes. A total of 56 images and 10 images were used for the training and the test sets, respectively. Images in the training set take the following name structure: [1-14].png corresponds to class 1, [15-28].png to class 2, [29-42].png to class 3, and [43-56].png to class 4. On the other hand, images in the test set are characterized by the word unknown followed by a number, for example, unknown1.png.

The images of the four classes have been extracted from the **Amsterdam Library of Object Images (ALOI)** available at `http://aloi.science.uva.nl/`.

Classes selected for the SVM classification example

The `SVMClassifier` **sample code is as follows:**

```
//… (omitted for simplicity)
#include <opencv2/features2d/features2d.hpp>
#include <opencv2/nonfree/features2d.hpp>

using namespace std;
using namespace cv;

int main(int argc, char *argv[]){

    Mat groups;
    Mat samples;
    vector<KeyPoint> keypoints1;
    //ORB feature detector with 15 interest points
    OrbFeatureDetector detector(15, 1.2f, 2, 31,0, 2,
      ORB::HARRIS_SCORE, 31);
    Mat descriptors, descriptors2;
    //SURF feature descriptor
    SurfDescriptorExtractor extractor;

    //Training samples
    for(int i=1; i<=56; i++){
        stringstream nn;
```

```
        nn <<i<<".png";
        //Read the image to be trained
        Mat img=imread(nn.str());
        cvtColor(img, img, COLOR_BGR2GRAY);
        //Detect interest points
        detector.detect(img, keypoints1);
        //Compute SURF descriptors
        extractor.compute(img, keypoints1, descriptors);
        //Organize and save information in one row
        samples.push_back(descriptors.reshape(1,1));
        keypoints1.clear();
    }

    //Set the labels of each sample
    for(int j=1; j<=56; j++){
        if(j<=14)  groups.push_back(1);
        else if(j>14 && j<=28)  groups.push_back(2);
            else if(j>28 && j<=42)  groups.push_back(3);
                else groups.push_back(4);
    }

    //Indicate SVM parameters
    CvSVMParams params=CvSVMParams(CvSVM::C_SVC, CvSVM::LINEAR, 0, 1,
        0, 1, 0, 0, 0, cvTermCriteria(CV_TERMCRIT_ITER+CV_TERMCRIT_EPS,
        100, FLT_EPSILON));

    //Create SVM classifier
    CvSVM classifierSVM;

    //Train classifier
    classifierSVM.train(samples, groups, Mat(), Mat(), params );

    //Test samples
    for(int i=1; i<=10; i++){
        stringstream nn;
        nn <<"unknown"<<i<<".png";
        //Read the image to be tested
        Mat unknown=imread(nn.str());
        cvtColor(unknown, unknown, COLOR_BGR2GRAY);
        //Detect interest points
        detector.detect(unknown, keypoints1);
        //Compute descriptors
        extractor.compute(unknown, keypoints1, descriptors2);
```

```
        //Test sample
        float result=
          classifierSVM.predict(descriptors2.reshape(1,1));
        //Print result
        cout<<nn.str()<<": class "<<result<<endl;
    }
    return 0;
}
```

The explanation of the code is given as follows. In this example, images are represented by their descriptors (see *Chapter 5, Focusing on the Interesting 2D Features*). For each image in the training set, its interest points are detected using an **Oriented FAST and Rotated BRIEF (ORB)** detector (OrbFeatureDetector) and its descriptors are computed using the **Speeded Up Robust Features (SURF)** descriptor (SurfDescriptorExtractor).

An SVM classifier is created using the CvSVM class and its parameters are set using the CvSVMParams::CvSVMParams(int svm_type, int kernel_type, double degree, double gamma, double coef0, double Cvalue, double nu, double p, CvMat* class_weights, CvTermCriteria term_crit) constructor. The interesting parameters in this constructor are the type of SVM (svm_type) and the type of kernel (kernel_type). The first specified parameter takes, in our case, the CvSVM::C_SVC value because an n-classification ($n \geq 2$) with an imperfect separation of the classes is needed. It also uses a C penalty value for atypical values. C acts, therefore, as a regularizer. The kernel_type parameter indicates the type of SVM kernel. The kernel represents the basis function required to separate the cases. For the SVM classifier, OpenCV includes the following kernels:

- CvSVM::LINEAR: The linear kernel
- CvSVM::POLY: The polynomial kernel
- CvSVM::RBF: The radial basis function
- CvSVM::SIGMOID: The sigmoid kernel

Then, the classifier builds an optimal linear discriminating function using the training set (with the `train` function). Now, it is prepared to classify new unlabeled samples. The test set is used for this purpose. Note that we also have to calculate the ORB detector and the SURF descriptors for each image in the test set. The result is as shown in the following screenshot, where all the classes have been classified correctly:

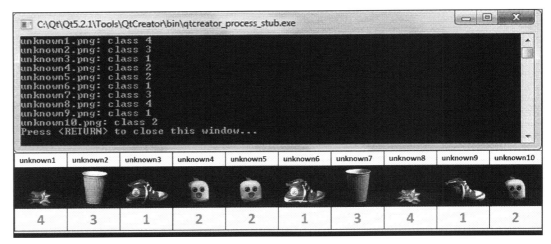

The classification result using SVM

What about GPUs?

CPUs seem to have reached their speed and thermal power limits. It has become complex and expensive to build a computer with several processors. Here is where GPUs come into play. **General-Purpose Computing on Graphics Processing Units (GPGPU)** is a new programming paradigm that uses the GPU to perform computations and enables the faster execution of programs and a reduction of power consumption. They include hundreds of general-purpose computing processors that can do much more than render graphics, especially if they are used in tasks that can be parallelized, which is the case with computer vision algorithms.

OpenCV includes support for the OpenCL and CUDA architectures, with the latter having more implemented algorithms and a better optimization. This is the reason why we are introducing the CUDA GPU module in this chapter.

Setting up OpenCV with CUDA

The installation guide presented in *Chapter 1, Getting Started*, needs a few additional steps in order to include the GPU module. We assume that the computer in which OpenCV is going to be installed already has the software detailed in that guide.

There are new requirements to be satisfied in order to compile OpenCV with CUDA on Windows:

- **CUDA-capable GPU**: This is the main requirement. Note that CUDA is developed by NVIDIA and, consequently, it is only compatible with NVIDIA graphic cards. Besides, the model of the card has to be listed at `http://developer.nvidia.com/cuda-gpus`. The so-called **Compute Capability (CC)** can also be checked on this website as it will be needed later.

- **Microsoft Visual Studio**: CUDA is compatible only with this Microsoft compiler. It is possible to install the Visual Studio Express edition, which is free. Note that Visual Studio 2013 is still not compatible with CUDA at the time of writing, so we are using Visual Studio 2012 in this book.

- **NVIDIA CUDA Toolkit**: This includes a compiler for GPUs, libraries, tools, and documentation. This toolkit is available at `https://developer.nvidia.com/cuda-downloads`.

- **Qt library for Visual C++ compiler**: In *Chapter 1*, *Getting Started*, the MinGW binaries of the Qt library were installed, but they are not compatible with the Visual C++ compiler. A compatible version can be downloaded using the package manager by means of the `MaintenanceTool` application located in `C:\Qt`. A good choice is the `msvc2012` 32-bit component, as can be seen in the following screenshot. It is also necessary to update the `Path` environment with the new location (for example, in our local system, it is `C:\Qt\5.2.1\msvc2012\bin`). The Qt library is included in the compilation to take advantage of its user interface features.

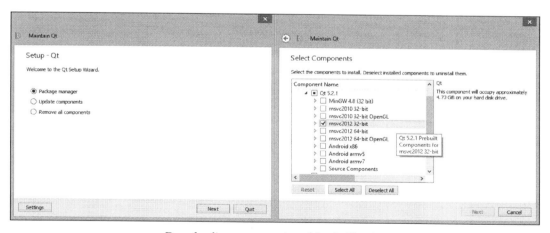

Downloading a new version of the Qt libraries

Configuring the OpenCV build

The build configuration with CMake differs in some points from the typical one explained in the first chapter. These differences are explained as follows:

- When you select the generator for the project, you have to choose the Visual Studio compiler version that corresponds to the installed environment in the machine. In our case, Visual Studio 11 is the correct compiler, as it corresponds to the version of the compiler included in Visual Studio 2012. The following screenshot shows this selection.

- In the selection of build options, we have to focus on the CUDA-related ones. If the installation of the CUDA toolkit was correct, CMake should automatically detect its location and activate the `WITH_CUDA` option. In addition, the installation path of the toolkit is shown through `CUDA_TOOLKIT_ROOT_DIR`. Another interesting option is `CUDA_ARCH_BIN` because the compilation time can be significantly reduced if we just select the corresponding version of our GPU; otherwise, it will compile the code for all the architectures. As mentioned previously, the version can be checked at `http://developer.nvidia.com/cuda-gpus`. The following screenshot shows the options set in our build configuration:

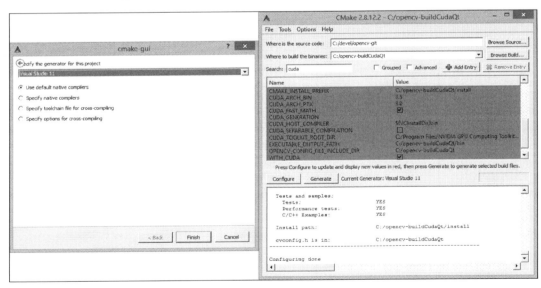

The CMake build configuration

Building and installing the library

CMake generates several Visual Studio projects in the target directory, ALL_BUILD being the essential one. Once it is opened in Visual Studio, we can choose the build configuration (Debug or Release) as well as the architecture (Win32 or Win64). The compilation starts by pressing *F7* or by clicking on **Build Solution**. After the compilation has finished, it is recommended that you open and build the INSTALL project as it generates an install directory with all the necessary files.

Finally, the Path system needs to be updated with the location of the newly generated binaries. It is important to remove the previous location from the Path variable and have only one version of the binaries in it.

 Qt Creator should now find two compilers and two Qt versions: one for Visual C++ and one for MingGW. We have to choose the correct kit depending on the developed application when creating a new project. It is also possible to change the configuration of an existing project as kits are manageable.

A quick recipe for setting up OpenCV with CUDA

The installation process can be summarized in the following steps:

1. Install Microsoft Visual Studio Express 2012.

2. Download and install the NVIDIA CUDA Toolkit (available at https://developer.nvidia.com/cuda-downloads).

3. Add the binaries for the Visual C++ compiler to the Qt installation and update the Path system with the new location (for example, C:\Qt\5.2.1\msvc2012\bin).

4. Configure the OpenCV build with CMake. Set the WITH_CUDA, CUDA_ARCH_BIN, WITH_QT, and BUILD_EXAMPLES options.

5. Open the ALL_BUILD Visual Studio project and build it. Do the same operation with the INSTALL project.

6. Modify the Path environment variable to update the OpenCV bin directory (for example, C:\opencv-buildCudaQt\install\x86\vc11\bin).

Our first GPU-based program

In this section, we show two versions of the same program: one version uses the CPU to perform computations, and the other version uses the GPU. These two examples are called `edgesCPU` and `edgesGPU`, respectively, and allow us to point out the differences when using the GPU module in OpenCV.

The `edgesCPU` example is presented in the first place:

```
#include <iostream>
#include "opencv2/core/core.hpp"
#include "opencv2/highgui/highgui.hpp"
#include "opencv2/imgproc/imgproc.hpp"
using namespace cv;

int main(int argc, char** argv){
if ( argc < 2 ){
        std::cout << "Usage: ./edgesGPU <image>" << std::endl;
        return -1;
    }
    Mat orig = imread(argv[1]);
    Mat gray, dst;

    bilateralFilter(orig,dst,-1,50,7);
    cvtColor(dst,gray,COLOR_BGR2GRAY);
    Canny(gray,gray,7,20);

    imshow("Canny Filter", gray);
    waitKey(0);

    return 0;
}
```

Now the `edgesGPU` example is shown as follows:

```
#include <iostream>
#include <opencv2/core/core.hpp>
#include <opencv2/highgui/highgui.hpp>
#include <opencv2/gpu/gpu.hpp>
using namespace cv;

int main( int argc, char** argv){
  if ( argc < 2 ){
```

```
                    std::cout << "Usage: ./edgesGPU <image>" << std::endl;
                    return -1;
            }
            Mat orig = imread(argv[1]);
            gpu::GpuMat g_orig, g_gray, g_dst;
            //Transfer the image data to the GPU
            g_orig.upload(orig);

            gpu::bilateralFilter(g_orig,g_dst,-1,50,7);
            gpu::cvtColor(g_dst,g_gray,COLOR_BGR2GRAY);
            gpu::Canny(g_gray,g_gray,7,20);

            Mat dst;
            //Copy the image back to the CPU memory
            g_gray.download(dst);
            imshow("Canny Filter", dst);
            waitKey(0);

            return 0;
    }
```

The explanation of the code is given as follows. There are several differences in the previous examples, although they ultimately obtain the same result, as shown in the following screenshot. A new header file is added as the new data type and different implementations of the algorithms are used. `#include <opencv2/gpu/gpu.hpp>` contains the GpuMat data type, which is the basic container that stores images in the GPU memory. It also includes the specific GPU versions of the filter algorithms used in the second example.

An important consideration is that we need to transfer the images between the CPU and the GPU. This is achieved with the g_orig.upload(orig) and g_gray. download(dst) methods. Once the image is uploaded to the GPU, we can apply different operations to it that are executed on the GPU. In order to distinguish the version of the algorithm that needs to run, the gpu namespace is used as in gpu::bilateralFilter, gpu::cvtColor, and gpu::Canny. After the filters have been applied, the image is copied to the CPU memory again and displayed.

Regarding performance, the CPU version runs in 297 milliseconds, whereas the GPU version runs in just 18 milliseconds. In other words, the GPU version runs 16.5x faster.

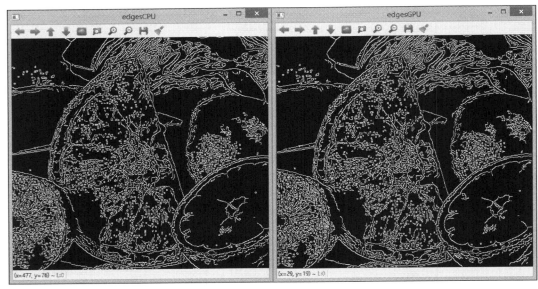

The output of the edgesCPU and edgesGPU examples

Going real time

One of the main advantages of using the GPU to perform computations in images is that they are much faster. This increase in speed allows you to run heavy computational algorithms in real-time applications, such as stereo vision, pedestrian detection, or dense optical flow. In the next `matchTemplateGPU` example, we show an application that matches a template in a video sequence:

```
#include <iostream>
#include "opencv2/core/core.hpp"
#include "opencv2/highgui/highgui.hpp"
#include "opencv2/features2d/features2d.hpp"
#include "opencv2/gpu/gpu.hpp"
#include "opencv2/nonfree/gpu.hpp"

using namespace std;
using namespace cv;

int main( int argc, char** argv )
```

```
{
    Mat img_template_cpu = imread( argv[1],IMREAD_GRAYSCALE);
    gpu::GpuMat img_template;
    img_template.upload(img_template_cpu);

    //Detect keypoints and compute descriptors of the template
    gpu::SURF_GPU surf;
    gpu::GpuMat keypoints_template, descriptors_template;

    surf(img_template,gpu::GpuMat(),keypoints_template,
      descriptors_template);

    //Matcher variables
    gpu::BFMatcher_GPU matcher(NORM_L2);

    //VideoCapture from the webcam
    gpu::GpuMat img_frame;
    gpu::GpuMat img_frame_gray;
    Mat img_frame_aux;
    VideoCapture cap;
    cap.open(0);
    if (!cap.isOpened()){
        cerr << "cannot open camera" << endl;
        return -1;
    }
    int nFrames = 0;
    uint64 totalTime = 0;
    //main loop
    for(;;){
        int64 start = getTickCount();
        cap >> img_frame_aux;
        if (img_frame_aux.empty())
            break;
        img_frame.upload(img_frame_aux);
        cvtColor(img_frame,img_frame_gray, CV_BGR2GRAY);

        //Step 1: Detect keypoints and compute descriptors
        gpu::GpuMat keypoints_frame, descriptors_frame;
        surf(img_frame_gray,gpu::GpuMat(),keypoints_frame,
          descriptors_frame);

        //Step 2: Match descriptors
        vector<vector<DMatch>>matches;
        matcher.knnMatch(descriptors_template,
          descriptors_frame,matches,2);

        //Step 3: Filter results
```

```
vector<DMatch> good_matches;
float ratioT = 0.7;
for(int i = 0; i < (int) matches.size(); i++)
{
    if((matches[i][0].distance <
      ratioT*(matches[i][1].distance)) && ((int)
        matches[i].size()<=2 && (int)
          matches[i].size()>0))
    {
        good_matches.push_back(matches[i][0]);
    }
}
// Step 4: Download results
vector<KeyPoint> keypoints1, keypoints2;
vector<float> descriptors1, descriptors2;
surf.downloadKeypoints(keypoints_template, keypoints1);
surf.downloadKeypoints(keypoints_frame, keypoints2);
surf.downloadDescriptors(descriptors_template, descriptors1);
surf.downloadDescriptors(descriptors_frame, descriptors2);

//Draw the results
Mat img_result_matches;
drawMatches(img_template_cpu, keypoints1, img_frame_aux,
  keypoints2, good_matches, img_result_matches);
imshow("Matching a template", img_result_matches);

int64 time_elapsed = getTickCount() - start;
double fps = getTickFrequency() / time_elapsed;
totalTime += time_elapsed;
nFrames++;
cout << "FPS : " << fps <<endl;

int key = waitKey(30);
if (key == 27)
    break;;
}
double meanFps = getTickFrequency() / (totalTime / nFrames);
cout << "Mean FPS: " << meanFps << endl;

return 0;
}
```

The explanation of the code is given as follows. As detailed in *Chapter 5, Focusing on the Interesting 2D Features*, features can be used to find the correspondence between two images. The template image, which is searched afterwards within every frame, is processed in the first place using the GPU version of SURF (`gpu::SURF_GPU surf;`) to detect interest points and extract descriptors. This is accomplished by running `surf(img_template,gpu::GpuMat(),keypoints_template, descriptors_template);`. The same process is performed for every frame taken from the video sequence. In order to match the descriptors of both images, a GPU version of the BruteForce matcher is also created with `gpu::BFMatcher_GPU matcher(NORM_L2);`. An extra step is needed due to the fact that interest points and descriptors are stored in the GPU memory, and they need to be downloaded before we can show them. That's why `surf.downloadKeypoints(keypoints, keypoints);` and `surf.downloadDescriptors(descriptors, descriptors);` are executed. The following screenshot shows the example running:

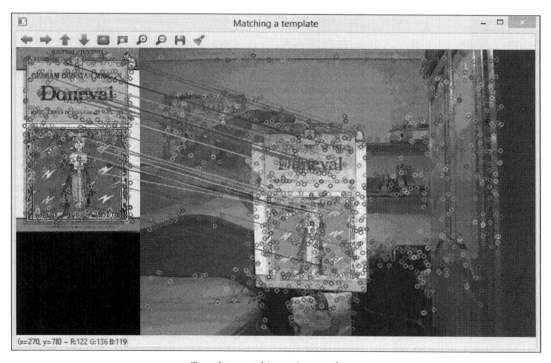

Template matching using a webcam

Performance

The principal motivation for choosing GPU programming is performance. Therefore, this example includes time measurements to compare the speedups obtained with respect to the CPU version. Specifically, time is saved at the beginning of the main loop of the program by means of the `getTickCount()` method. At the end of this loop, the same method is used as well as `getTickFrequency`, which helps to calculate the FPS of the current frame. The time elapsed in each frame is accumulated, and at the end of the program, the mean is computed. The previous example has an average latency of 15 FPS, whereas the same example using CPU data types and algorithms achieves a mere 0.5 FPS. Both examples have been tested on the same hardware: a PC equipped with an i5-4570 processor and an NVIDIA GeForce GTX 750 graphics card. Obviously, a speed increment of 30x is significant, especially when we just need to change a few lines of code.

Summary

In this chapter, we have covered two advanced modules of OpenCV: machine learning and GPU. Machine learning has the capability to learn computers to make decisions. For this, a classifier is trained and validated. This chapter provides three classification samples: KNN classifier, Random Forest using a `.cvs` database, and SVM using an image database. The chapter also addresses the use of OpenCV with CUDA. GPUs have a growing role in intensive tasks because they can offload the CPU and run parallel tasks such as those encountered in computer vision algorithms. Several GPU examples have been provided: GPU module installation, a basic first GPU program, and real-time template matching.

What else?

The GPU module now covers most of the functionalities of OpenCV; so, it is recommended that you explore the library and check which algorithms are available. In addition, the `performance_gpu` program can be found at `[opencv_build]/install/x86/vc11/samples/gpu]`, which shows the speedups of many OpenCV algorithms when using the GPU version.

Index

W

X

Thank you for buying
OpenCV Essentials

About Packt Publishing

Packt, pronounced 'packed', published its first book "*Mastering phpMyAdmin for Effective MySQL Management*" in April 2004 and subsequently continued to specialize in publishing highly focused books on specific technologies and solutions.

Our books and publications share the experiences of your fellow IT professionals in adapting and customizing today's systems, applications, and frameworks. Our solution based books give you the knowledge and power to customize the software and technologies you're using to get the job done. Packt books are more specific and less general than the IT books you have seen in the past. Our unique business model allows us to bring you more focused information, giving you more of what you need to know, and less of what you don't.

Packt is a modern, yet unique publishing company, which focuses on producing quality, cutting-edge books for communities of developers, administrators, and newbies alike. For more information, please visit our website: www.packtpub.com.

About Packt Open Source

In 2010, Packt launched two new brands, Packt Open Source and Packt Enterprise, in order to continue its focus on specialization. This book is part of the Packt Open Source brand, home to books published on software built around Open Source licenses, and offering information to anybody from advanced developers to budding web designers. The Open Source brand also runs Packt's Open Source Royalty Scheme, by which Packt gives a royalty to each Open Source project about whose software a book is sold.

Writing for Packt

We welcome all inquiries from people who are interested in authoring. Book proposals should be sent to author@packtpub.com. If your book idea is still at an early stage and you would like to discuss it first before writing a formal book proposal, contact us; one of our commissioning editors will get in touch with you.

We're not just looking for published authors; if you have strong technical skills but no writing experience, our experienced editors can help you develop a writing career, or simply get some additional reward for your expertise.

Android Application Programming with OpenCV

ISBN: 978-1-84969-520-6   Paperback: 130 pages

Build Android apps to capture, manipulate, and track objects in 2D and 3D

1. Set up OpenCV and an Android development environment on Windows, Mac, or Linux.

2. Capture and display real-time videos and still images.

3. Manipulate image data using OpenCV and Apache Commons Math.

4. Track objects and render 2D and 3D graphics on top of them.

OpenCV Computer Vision with Python

ISBN: 978-1-78216-392-3   Paperback: 122 pages

Learn to capture videos, manipulate images, and track objects with Python using the OpenCV Library

1. Set up OpenCV, its Python bindings, and optional Kinect drivers on Windows, Mac, or Ubuntu.

2. Create an application that tracks and manipulates faces.

3. Identify face regions using normal color images and depth images.

Please check **www.PacktPub.com** for information on our titles

open source
community experience distilled

Instant OpenCV for iOS

ISBN: 978-1-78216-384-8   Paperback: 96 pages

Learn how to build real-time computer vision applications for the iOS platform using the OpenCV library

1. Learn something new in an Instant! A short, fast, focused guide delivering immediate results.

2. Build and run your OpenCV code on iOS.

3. Become familiar with iOS fundamentals and make your application interact with the GUI, camera, and gallery.

4. Build your library of computer vision effects, including photo and video filters.

Mastering OpenCV with Practical Computer Vision Projects

ISBN: 978-1-84951-782-9   Paperback: 340 pages

Step-by-step tutorials to solve common real-world computer vision problems for desktop or mobile, from augmented reality and number plate recognition to face recognition and 3D head tracking

1. Allows anyone with basic OpenCV experience to rapidly obtain skills in many computer vision topics, for research or commercial use.

2. Each chapter is a separate project covering a computer vision problem, written by a professional with proven experience on that topic.

3. All projects include a step-by-step tutorial and full source-code, using the C++ interface of OpenCV.

Please check **www.PacktPub.com** for information on our titles

16603391R00119

Printed in Great Britain
by Amazon